E. J. LANGFORD GARSTIN

THEURGY

OR THE

HERMETIC PRACTICE

A Treatise on Spiritual Alchemy

Martino Publishing
Mansfield Centre, CT
2012

Martino Publishing
P.O. Box 373,
Mansfield Centre, CT 06250 USA

www.martinopublishing.com

ISBN   978-1-61427-344-8

© *2012 Martino Publishing*

Cover design by T. Matarazzo

Printed in the United States of America On 100% Acid-Free Paper

E. J. LANGFORD GARSTIN

THEURGY

OR THE

HERMETIC PRACTICE

A Treatise on Spiritual Alchemy

1930
LONDON: RIDER & CO.
Paternoster House, E.C.4

Printed in Great Britain at
The Mayflower Press, Plymouth. William Brendon & Son, Ltd.

PREFACE

THE title selected for this short treatise may at first sight appear to be either very ambitious or presumptuous or even both. Alternatively it may be held to be misleading on the ground that this is not really a practical textbook.

It would therefore appear advisable, from the very start, to warn the intending reader that no claim is made herein to any special knowledge of the Art other than that which can be gleaned from the careful study of the published works of the Alchemical writers, and the use of such powers of insight and intuition regarding their admittedly involved and cryptic phraseology as the author may possess.

Of necessity various subjects usually classed under the general heading of Occultism will have to be considered, and some preliminary remarks under this head may not be inappropriate.

Many people fight shy of Occultism because of its undesirable associations in their minds with credulity and superstition, neurotics and hysteria, charlatanry and fraud, and because they are accustomed to regard what genuine residuum there may be left as consisting in undesirable and dangerous practices.

On reflection, however, it will be found that the

same impression is prevalent *in toto* among many regarding Spiritualism, and in part regarding Mysticism, while the Orthodox Religions do not escape altogether scatheless.

It is not intended herein to indulge in apologetics on behalf of Occultism, which, divested of the illusions held about it, is quite capable of speaking for itself as it were, and requires no defence. It is merely proposed to discuss what is termed Theurgia, which is the practical part of Spiritual Alchemy, as far as the limits of space and the avoidance of undue technicalities will permit.

Theurgy, defined a little more carefully, means "The Science or Art of Divine Works," and it is the same as the Telestic or Perfecting Work. In Alchemy it is called the "Great Work," which is the purification and exaltation of the lower nature by the proper application of scientific principles, so that it may become united with its higher counterparts, whereby the individual may attain to Spiritual, and ultimately Divine, Consciousness.

By scientific principles are to be understood "known principles," though the fact that these are not generally known is the origin of the term "occult," which merely means, according to the dictionary, "escaping observation, not discovered without test or experiment," which definitions apply with equal force to any department of scientific research.

6

PREFACE

Were this definition more commonly recognised, it is possible that there would be less misleading talk and less misunderstanding on the part of the opponents of the Arcane Sciences than there are at present, and that there would not be so much condemnation where there has been no previous careful investigation.

We would also say a word by way of apology to the reader who may feel that we have made too lavish a use of quotations. Our object is twofold. Firstly, that no one may imagine that they have to rely merely upon the speculations of some dilettante dabbler in the Occult Sciences, but that they may see for themselves the sources from which our conclusions are drawn. Secondly, because we feel unable to improve upon the sayings of these writers, save only by bringing together the references that are not merely scattered through their various works, but also, on their own confession, placed very often out of their proper sequence and relationship even in their individual books. Passages thus correlated often assume fresh importance, and from them, sometimes, the unexpected truth emerges. If we have to any extent succeeded in thus throwing light upon the sayings of the sages, however little it may be, we shall have more than achieved our object.

THEURGY

CHAPTER I

THEURGY, or the Telestic Work, was the very essence of the teaching of the Mystery Schools of Egypt, of Samothrace and of Eleusis ; of Zoroaster, of Mithra and of Orpheus. And in Egypt, the cradle of them all, were initiated many of the outstanding men of their day, such as Pythagoras, Plato, Demokritos, Eudoxus, Archimedes, Chrysippos, Euripides, Proklos, Thales and many others.

In addition many of the Fathers of the Church, such as Clement of Alexandria, Cyrillus and Synesius, were also initiated into the Mysteries and regarded them as sacred and efficacious, transferring in part the very language, rites and disciplines of them to their own forms of worship, as is even to-day apparent.

Proklos tells us that " The Perfective Rite leads the way as the muesis or mystic initiation, and after that is the epopteia or beholding."

Plato calls Zoroastrian Magic " The Service of the

Gods," and Psellus affirms that " Its function is to initiate or perfect the human soul by the power of materials here on earth, for the supreme faculty of the soul cannot by its own guidance aspire to the sublimest intuitions, and to the comprehension of Divinity."

Clement of Alexandria alludes to the Mysteries as Blessed and says : " O Mysteries truly Sacred ! O pure light ! At the light of the torches the veil that covers Deity and Heaven falls off. I am Holy now that I am initiated." While Synesius, speaking in alchemical terms, declares that " the Quintessence is no other than our viscous, celestial and glorious soul, drawn from its minera by our magistery."

Nor are the later students and masters of the art less well known, for included among their number were such men as Appollonius of Tyana, Albertus Magnus, Roger Bacon, Paracelsus, Arnold de Villa Nova, Picus di Mirandola, Trithemius, Boehme, Cornelius Agrippa and many others.

But to leave the historical aspect, which, however interesting, is relatively unimportant, and to come to our subject, Theurgy is inextricably associated with Religion ; is, in fact, its very kernel ; for on investigation we find that beneath the exoteric and allegorical forms of all ancient doctrines, and hidden carefully within all their sacred writings, there is an underlying principle which is in every case the same, but is yet invariably concealed in one way or another.

THEURGY

This central teaching deals with rebirth, or birth from above, and, if we are to believe the records of antiquity, there is, and always has been, a definite body of scientific teaching on this subject, the knowledge of which, though jealously guarded, was never denied to the genuine and earnest seeker.

Unfortunately the mental and spiritual limitations of the vast bulk of mankind throughout the ages have always prevented the public teaching of this science, and necessitated the maintenance of the strictest secrecy, the knowledge being invariably given in the involved, complicated and envious language of symbol and allegory.

· This is, of course, a constant source of annoyance to many people to-day, who declare themselves as being opposed on principle to what they term " artificial secrecy " in any shape or form ; and to an even larger number, who, being without any particular principles, are decidedly averse from undertaking the necessary labour, but desire a clear exposition in "popular" form.

As Mrs. Atwood, in her *Suggestive Enquiry*, very succinctly puts it : " No such alluring baits to idleness are to be found on the title pages of the middle age school of philosophy ; no such simplifications of science as we now hear of are belonging to Alchemy. It is true, there are Revelations, Open Entrances, New Lights and True Lights, Sunshine and Moonshine, with other Auroras and pictured Dawns ; Manuals,

THEURGY

Introductory Lexicons of obscure terms, with meanings no less obscured ; Triumphal Chariots also, Banners, Gates, Keys and Guides, too, without number, all directing on the same Royal Road when this is found ; but useless to most wayfarers ; nothing that we observe at all suited to the means or taste of the millionaire class of readers, whose understanding, like that of pampered children, has grown flaccid ; and by excess of object-teaching, has forgotten how to think."

As for the complaint of the others, it is difficult to understand what is meant by " artificial secrecy " unless it means making a secret out of nothing, or pretending to have some secret information, when in point of fact one has none—a charge which has for long been unjustly laid against the Alchemists. If this be the meaning of the phrase we cannot but be heartily in agreement with it, but if it means the deliberate with-holding of certain knowledge from the masses, then it entirely depends on the reasons that can be given for the secrecy as to whether the term " artificial " is justifiable.

Now if the object of Theurgy and Spiritual Alchemy be solely the purification and exaltation of the Soul, it may be argued that such knowledge ought to be broad-casted and not obscured ; that it is obviously for the good of mankind, and that to conceal it is virtually criminal.

THEURGY

But it must be remembered that what is proposed is a method of accelerated Soul development by a system of intensive culture, as is in many places asserted; and it would appear that there is every reason why those who were in possession of the requisite knowledge were chary of passing it on. And these reasons, when we examine them, must apply equally forcibly to-day for those, if such there be, who are the guardians of the secret.

For the practice of this art opens up very dangerous possibilities, involving, as it is said to do, an understanding of the working and application of certain arcane forces of nature, commonly called magic.

Now magic is a purely relative term, the magic of antiquity, or some of it, being the common knowledge of to-day. But knowledge is power, and power can always be used in two ways, for good or for evil. We have only to look around us to see the appalling results of an unwise dissemination of knowledge, seeing that man is almost invariably tempted, and almost as invariably succumbs to the temptation to use his knowledge for purely personal and material ends, and very often for destruction. For which reason it may well be submitted that there is at least an excellent prima facie case for secrecy.

This at any rate was the conviction of the Alchemists, as witness that saying of Raymund Lully, " I swear to

13

thee upon my soul that thou art damned if thou shouldst reveal these things. For every good thing proceeds from God and to Him only is due. Wherefore thou shalt reserve and keep secret that which God only should reveal, and thou shalt affirm thou dost justly keep back those things whose revelation is to His honour. For if thou shouldst reveal that in a few words which God hath been forming a long time, thou shouldst be condemned in the great day of judgement as a traitor to the majesty of God, neither should thy treason be forgiven thee. For the revelation of such things belongs to God and not to man."

Justified or not, however, the secrecy exists, and it may well be asked where clues may best be sought, which may be followed in the search for this jealously guarded wisdom.

The answer would appear to be that such clues are to be found almost anywhere in the religious, philosophical and mystical writings of either the East or the West, but that it will probably come more easily to the majority of Westerners to take the Egyptian, Semitic and Greek and not the Eastern systems. For this reason, therefore, a study of certain books of the Bible, notably the Pentateuch, Solomon, Job, Ezekiel, the Gospels, the Epistles of St. Paul and the Revelation of St. John, will be found profitable, especially if the student be aided by some knowledge of the Qabalah, which is the great key to their understanding. Among the uncanonical books Enoch and Wisdom are helpful, and apart from these Semitic writings, the so-called Egyptian Book of the Dead, the works of many of the Greek Philosophers, the Gnostic and Hermetic fragments, expositions of the Mysteries, especially Iamblichos, and almost all the Alchemical writers, are full of illumination.

Of the three sources mentioned above, Egyptian, Semitic and Greek, the first is unquestionably the most ancient, but Egypt has left but few traces for us. The Jews derived their knowledge primarily from her through Moses, whatever they may have adopted subsequently from Chaldean, Babylonian and other sources, while even the Greeks obtained much of their inspiration and actual knowledge from her Mystery Schools.

Thus, therefore, is it that the Qabalah, the Jewish Mystical tradition, which was handed on orally for centuries, and was not written down till some as yet undetermined date in our era, forms one of the principal keys, not merely to the Jewish and Christian Scriptures, but to all the other sources we have mentioned ; for the language of symbol and allegory is an universal language, and the student will observe for himself that many of the Alchemical writers were avowed Qabalists.

As, however, the Qabalah is a highly technical subject, and as it is proposed to avoid technicalities as

15

far as may be, direct allusions to it will be as few as possible in the pages which follow.

With all the mass of clues which surround us everywhere when we begin seriously to look for them, it is difficult to know where to make a start, for to review them all would take volumes. Still, as the science of the ancients was a causal science and reasoned from universals to particulars, it will be best to pick on some symbol of the Universe, and then to seek its counterpart in ourselves, whereby we may glean some idea of what was to be achieved, and afterwards to take some other clue, which may lead us to an understanding of how it was to be done.

Nevertheless, as our quest is concerned primarily with the Soul, we will first of all devote ourselves to a consideration of some of the views held by the ancients regarding it.

CHAPTER II

WHEREVER we direct our attention in the physical or spiritual worlds, we are likely to encounter an apparent paradox, and it should, therefore, cause us no surprise that in considering the Soul we immediately find such a state of affairs existing.

We are accustomed to the idea that man is not a simple being; that he is composed of body and soul, or even of body, soul and spirit, though there appears to be considerable looseness in the way these two latter terms are used.

We also admit that the soul is the principal part of man; is, in fact, the man himself, leaving on one side for the moment the differentiation between soul and spirit. But we find it difficult to grasp that the soul is at once indivisible and divisible; that it is both one and yet possessing parts.

Nevertheless this hypothesis underlies the teaching of the Egyptians, Hebrews and Greeks, whom we are principally considering, and we are compelled to form some coherent view of the divisions of the soul if we are to follow the writings wherein we propose to look for our clues.

B

THEURGY

It will perhaps be simpler to consider first some of the Qabalistic ideas concerning the Soul, for they possess a quite definite terminology which is missing in many of the others. This will furnish us with a standard of comparison and of correspondence that should be distinctly useful.

According to the Zohar, the Soul was divided into three parts, of which the highest was termed Neshamah, corresponding to the intellectual world; the second Ruach, the seat of good and evil, corresponding to the moral world; and the third, Nephesch, the animal life and desires, corresponding to the material world of sense.

Now Neshamah was itself divided into three parts, for, as the highest part of the soul, it represented what was termed the Supernal Triad, composed of the first three Sephiroth or Emanations.

It is here necessary to digress for a moment to explain that the system of the Qabalah postulates the existence of ten Sephiroth—which may be regarded either as Emanations from, or the Highest Abstract Ideas of, God—conformed into four Worlds called Atziluth, Briah, Yetzirah and Assiah, which are respectively Archetypal or pure Deity, Creative, Formative and Material. The first Sephira comprises the first World, that of Atziluth, the next two that of Briah, the next six that of Yetzirah, and the last that of Assiah.

THEURGY

The Supernal Triad, therefore, mentioned above, being composed of the first three Sephiroth, embraces the first two Worlds, and the three divisions of Neshamah, which are called Yechidah, Chiah and Neshamah respectively, are referred, the first to Atziluth and the next two to Briah.

The first of these conveys, therefore, the illimitable and transcendental idea of the Great Absolute and Incomprehensible One in the Soul. This is linked by Chiah, which suggests the idea of Essential Being, with Neshamah, and these two represent together Wisdom and Understanding, the higher governing, creative idea, the aspiration to the Ineffable One in the Soul.

Neshamah in turn links these Supernals with the Ruach, a word which means Spirit, and is here the Mind, the Reasoning Power, that which possesses the knowledge of good and of evil. It is to be noted carefully that this is the rational or discursive mind, and not the higher mind, which is represented by Neshamah.

Lastly we have the Nephesch, which is that power in the Soul which represents the passions and physical appetites.

The Zohar, Part II, fol. 94b, tells us that at birth man receives the Animal Soul (Nephesch), and if he is worthy, the Ruach or Intellectual Spirit. Lastly, if he is still more worthy, Neshamah, the Soul emanating from the Celestial Throne (by which is meant the

Briatic World). We need not, however, enter into a consideration of the possibility of man without the Ruach, or his nature, but will make the justifiable assumption that for all practical purposes man, according to the Qabalah, consists of Body, Nephesch and Ruach, that is Body, Soul and Spirit.

Among the Greeks Plato also makes a triple division, as does Plotinus, though others, as for example the Pythagorean Philolaus, give four.

We will take the Platonic system as being, probably, the most widely known and most often quoted. He gives the Nous or higher mind ; the phren or thumos, the lower mind, including, according to some, the psychic nature ; and the epithumia, comprising the emotional nature and the animal desires, appetites and passions. The faculties of the lower and higher minds he sub-divides into four, two to each. To the lower he allots Eikasia, the perception of images, and Pistis, faith and a sort of psychic groping after truth. To the higher he refers Dianoia, or philosophic reasoning, and Noesis, or direct cognition. The first two are amalgamated under the heading of Doxa, opinion or mostly illusory knowledge, while the other two are classed as Gnosis or Episteme, wisdom or true knowledge.

The first of the two sub-divisions of Doxa includes the whole of that body of knowledge which we term the inductive, physical sciences, these being concerned

20

exclusively with the observation and investigation of the phenomena of the material universe. The second embraces the numerous forms of dogmatic creeds and beliefs summed up as a rule as exoteric religion.

Of the two grades of Gnosis, the first refers to those more speculative aspects of philosophy, wherein an attempt is made to arrive at a knowledge of first principles by means of pure reasoning, while the second grade implies the power of the mind directly to apprehend the truth without going through any intermediate process of reasoning.

Comparing this system with that of the Qabalah, we observe that the Nous corresponds with the Neshamah, the Phren with the Ruach and the Epithumia with the Nephesch.

Regarding the allocation of the four faculties of the lower and higher minds, the reader may feel a little doubtful as to the allocation of the philosophical reason to the higher mind or Nous, which, from its very name, is definitely associated with the noetic or epistemonic faculty of direct perception of the truth ; but such questions are, after all, of relatively small importance.

Similar to the ideas we have outlined above are the following passages from Abammon's reply to Porphyry (Iamblichos de Mysteriis) when alluding to the Hermetic concepts. He says : " For man, as these writings affirm, has two souls. The one is from the First

Intelligence, and is participant of the power of the Creator, but the other is given from the revolutions of the worlds of the sky, to which the God-beholding soul returns. . . . But the Soul that is in its higher mental quality from the world of Intelligence, is superior to the movement of the world of generated existence, and through this there takes place both the unbinding of fate and the upward progress to the gods of the World of Mind.

" The Theurgic discipline, so far as it conducts upward to the Unbegotten, is made complete by a life of this kind. . . . For the soul has a principle of its own leading around to the realm of Intelligence, and not only standing aloof from things of the world of generated existence, but also joining it to that which is, even to the divine nature . . . (and) there is another principle of the soul which is superior to the whole realm of nature and generated existence. By it we can be united to the gods, rise above the established order of the world, and likewise participate in the life eternal and in the energy of the gods of the highest heaven. Through this principle we are able to set ourselves free."

Here, however, to make comparison with the Qabalistic ideas, we find allusion to the Ruach, to the Neshamah, and to a higher principle still, presumably the Yechidah. For the Ruach, as we have seen, corresponds to the Yetziratic or formative World, here alluded to as the " worlds of the sky," while Neshamah is the idea of wisdom and understanding, which, in our quotation, is "the higher mental quality from the world of Intelligence." But Abammon goes on to say that there is another principle beyond this, by which we participate in the eternal life and energy of the gods.

In conclusion, and as further illustrating the enormous importance attaching to the higher portion of the soul, the Neshamah, the Nous or the Mind, the following extracts are of interest, and it would perhaps be as well to point out here and now that none of these quotations is chosen merely to illustrate the point immediately under consideration, but all have their bearing on the telestic work.

The Zohar, Part I, fol. 246 (*La Kabbale*, Franck) says : " Come and see. Thought is the principle of all that is ; but it is at first Unknown and shut up in itself. When the Thought begins to develop itself forth, it arrives at that degree where it becomes Spirit. Arrived at this estate it takes the name of Intelligence, and is no longer as before it was, shut up in itself. The Spirit, in its turn, develops itself in the bosom of the mystery with which it is surrounded ; and there proceeds a voice which is the reunion of the celestial choirs, a voice that rolls forth in distinct utterance articulate, for It comes from the Mind."

In the Divine Poemander of Hermes Trismegistus, Book II, we find the following : " My thoughts being

once seriously busied about the things that be, and my
understanding lifted up—all my bodily senses being
utterly holden back; methought I saw one of an
exceedingly great stature and infinite greatness call me
by name, and say to me, What wouldst thou understand
to learn and know? Then said I, Who art thou? I
am, quoth he, Poemander, the Mind of the Great Lord,
the most mighty and absolute Emperor. I know what
thou wouldst have, and I am always present with thee
. . . I am that Light, the Mind, thy God, who am
before the moist nature that appeareth out of the
darkness, and that bright and lightful Word from the
Mind is the Son of God. How is that? quoth I. Thus,
replied he, understand it. That which, in thee,
seeth and heareth the Word of the Lord, and the
Mind, the Father, God, differ not from one another,
and the union of these is life . . . I, the mind, come into
men that are holy and good and pure and merciful, and
that live piously and religiously, and my presence is a
help unto them; and forthwith they know all things."

CHAPTER III

NOW at the end of Chapter I we proposed to select some symbol wherein we might look for a clue as to what was to be achieved, and in order that we may take some type that will be almost universally familiar, and at the same time find its parallel in Alchemical literature, we can hardly do better than choose one of the most ancient of all, the Serpent.

This symbol can be traced right back into the most remote ages, just as can Phallism, with which it is usually associated and allied. But it must not be thought for one moment that the latter was ever an integral part of the belief of the enlightened, or that they at any time worshipped serpents, though this accusation is quite frequently made against them. The fact is that Serpent Symbolism began to be misunderstood by the ignorant at a very early stage, the people having mistaken the symbol for the fact in a manner that has been emulated by their successors in the various religions of the world ever since.

What, then, is at the back of the Serpent Myths?

It is generally admitted that the Serpent was much used as a symbol for Wisdom, Creation, Generation and

Regeneration or Rebirth, and we shall do well to consider and correlate some of these ideas in order to see whether we may not, by such a study, discover the clue we are seeking. We will therefore take these four ideas seriatim, beginning with Wisdom.

Serpents have always been associated with Wisdom from the very earliest times, though side by side with them there have been " wicked serpents " and "crooked serpents " as their evil antitheses. To go no further than the Bible, we have Christ's injunction to the Apostles (Matt. x. 16), " Be ye therefore wise as serpents," which can mean no evil sort of knowledge ; over against which we have the first serpent mentioned in the Scriptures, the Serpent of the Fall, who was " more subtile than any beast of the field that the Lord God had made."

Then there were, on the one hand, the fiery serpents that afflicted the Children of Israel in the Wilderness, and on the other, the Brazen Serpent which Moses set upon a pole that the people might be perfectly healed. This latter is the Qabalistical Serpent of Wisdom, the Serpent Nogah, twined about the Central Pillar of the Sephirotic Tree (for the ten Sephiroth which we mentioned in Chapter II were arranged by the Qabalists in three Columns or Pillars, which arrangement was designated by them the Tree of Life), and is interpreted rightly or wrongly in Christian Symbolism as a type of Christ Crucified.

THEURGY

The bearing of this example on our subject is well illustrated by the following example of scriptural exegesis ascribed by Hippolytus to the Peratae, an otherwise unknown Gnostic School. It is admirably summarised by G. R. S. Mead, in his *Fragments of a Faith Forgotten.* He says:

"Thus then they explained the Exodus-myth. Egypt is the body; all those who identify themselves with the body are the ignorant, the Egyptians. To 'come forth' out of Egypt is to leave the body; and to pass through the Red Sea is to cross over the ocean of generation, the animal and sensual nature, which is hidden in the blood. Yet even then they are not safe; crossing the Red Sea they enter the Desert, the intermediate state of the doubting lower mind. There they are attacked by the 'gods of destruction,' which Moses called the 'serpents of the desert,' and which plague those who seek to escape from the 'gods of generation.' To them Moses, the teacher, shows the true serpent crucified on the cross of matter, and by its means they escape from the Desert and enter the promised land, the realm of the spiritual mind, where is the Heavenly Jordan, the World-Soul. When the Waters of Jordan flow downwards, then is the generation of men; but when they flow upwards, then is the creation of Gods."

Leaving the Bible we have the Winged Globe of Egypt, on many examples of which we may see the twin

27

serpents, leading us to the not unnatural inference that it was the prototype of the Caduceus of Hermes (who was, of course, the Egyptian Thoth), another form of the idea portrayed as the Tree of Life of the Qabalah.

Lest it be thought that we are getting away from the idea of Wisdom, it must be pointed out that the study and understanding of this Tree was the discovery of the True Wisdom, typified in the mystical Fifty Gates of Understanding of Binah, the third Sephira, the Mother Supernal, whose name signifies Understanding.

But as this point, Wisdom, will have to be stressed in two of the following sections, Creation and Regeneration or Rebirth, we will not pursue it further for the moment.

In the Creation Myth the evolution of the universe, according to some schools, followed the physical analogy of the generation of man in the womb from a " serpent " and an " egg." But the Cosmic serpent was variously described as the Great Power, the Illimitable Vortex, the Mighty Whirlwind, while the Egg figured as the Envelope embracing the All of the world system, as the primordial " fire-mist " which is still so familiar in modern theorisings. Taken thus, the Serpent was a type of the Will of God, Divine Intelligence, the Mind of the Father, the Word or Logos. The Egg represented the Primordial Idea, the Great Mother Supernal. The embryonic universe was

therefore portrayed as a circle, the Egg, with a serpent
either twined round it or placed diameter-wise across
it, representing the former of the Cosmos and of Man.
It was Man's Creator, but nevertheless it was supposed
that man could utilise the serpent force himself and
create by it; but first he must cease from generation
and free himself from its toils.

Before leaving this particular myth, let us see what
Thomas Vaughan in his *Magia Adamica*, when dealing
with the Egyptian Emepht, as he terms it—called
Emeph by Iamblichos—can tell us. Speaking of
Egyptian Theology he says :

"Their Catholic Doctrine, and wherein I find them
all to agree is this. Emepht, whereby they express
their Supreme God—and verily they mind the true
One—signifies properly an Intelligence or Spirit
converting all things into Himself and Himself into
all things. This is very sound Divinity and philosophy
if it be rightly understood. Now—say they—Emepht
produced an egg out of his mouth, which Kircher
expounds imperfectly, and withal erroneously. In the
production of this egg was manifested another Deity,
which they call Ptha, and out of some other natures
and substances enclosed in the egg, this Ptha formed
all things. But to deal a little more openly we will
describe unto you their hieroglyphic, wherein they have
very handsomely but obscurely discovered most of
their mysteries. First of all then, they draw a circle,

in the circle a serpent—not folded, but diameter-wise and at length. Her head resembles that of a hawk, the tail is tied in a small knot, and a little below the head her wings are volant. The circle points at Emepht, or God the Father, being infinite—without beginning, without end. Moreover, it comprehends or contains in itself the second Deity Ptha and the egg or chaos out of which all things were made.

" The Hawk in the Egyptian Symbols signifies light and spirit; his head annexed here to the serpent represents Ptha, or the Second Person, who is the First Light—as we have told you in our *Anthroposophia*. He is said to form all things out of the egg, because in Him—as it were in a glass—are certain types or images, namely, distinct conceptions of the Paternal Deity, according to which—by co-operation of the Spirit, namely, the Holy Ghost—the creatures are formed. The inferior part of the figure signifies the matter or chaos, which they call the egg of Emepht."

We must make a pause here before continuing with Thomas Vaughan, which we shall do a little further on, and consider briefly this name Emepht. According to Iamblichos it should be Emeph, and Wilder tells us that many have conjectured that this name should have been Kneph. This was the name of the Creator in Nubia and Elephantina, and He was considered to be the same as Amun, the Supreme God at Thebes. The name Kneph or Neph, he continues, almost identical with the Semitic term Nephesch or Soul, reminds us that this God was considered as the Soul of the World. Mariette-Bey considered him as the same as Thoth or Hermes, the God of learning. The Greeks, however, identified him with Asclepius, and the Orientals with Esmun of the Kabirian Rites.

Let us, however, hear Iamblichos himself on the subject.

"According to another arrangement," he says, "Hermes places the God Emeph as leader of the celestial Divinities, and declares that He is the Mind itself, perceptive of itself, and converting the perceptions into His own substance. But he places as prior to this divinity the One without specific parts, whom he affirms to be the first exemplar and whom he names Eikton. In him are the First Mind and the First Intelligence, and he is worshipped by Silence alone. Besides these, however, there are other leaders that preside over the creation of visible things. For the Creative Mind, guardian of Truth and Wisdom, coming to the realm of objective existence, and bringing the invisible power of occult words into light is called in the Egyptian language AMON (the Arcane): but as completing everything in a genuine manner without deceit and with skill, Phtha. The Greeks, however, assume Phtha to be the same as Hephaestos, giving their attention to the Creative art alone. But as the dispenser of benefits, he is called Osiris; and

31

by reason of his other powers and energies he has likewise other appellations."

Coming to our next section, Generation, we shall, if we are not careful, find ourselves wallowing in a morass of Phallism, for following the Hermetic Maxim, "As Above, so Below," the Serpent is used to illustrate both birth and rebirth by means of physical analogies with the material methods of reproduction.

The forces of sex, employed for their legitimate purpose, procreation, are manifestations on a lower plane of the great outpouring and energising of the creative Deity and the evolutionary processes of the cosmos. It need hardly be emphasised, however, that they are poles apart—as far removed from one another as is animal-human passion from Divine Will.

And the mysteries underlying these sex forces formed part of the curriculum laid down for the Aspirants of old, but the study of them was not lightly to be undertaken. They were rightly considered to be highly dangerous, for though an understanding of them might tend to a life of self-control and asceticism, a mere idle curiosity was likely to lead to the depths of depravity.

In this and what follows it may be as well to make it perfectly clear that nowhere in the truly sacred mysteries—at any rate of the West—was any teaching given involving any physical sex practices, such as attempted introversions of sexual forces, endeavouring to draw these up the spine and into the brain. In such directions lie disease, madness and death, and we cannot too strongly discourage anyone from being deluded enough to dabble with any such spurious and positively evil teachings, which, it is to be regretted, are current in many places to-day.

With this emphatic denial and warning we will continue.

For the purified in mind and body the reward was seership, illumination and direct or noetic knowledge, but for the impure there yawned that "precipice beneath the earth" of which the Oracle speaks.

Thus, almost invariably, we find in the history of such movements that the good and evil sides are found in close proximity, for the study of the mysteries of the self and of the cosmos leads naturally to a certain intensification of the whole nature, and if the animal and passional predominate it becomes even more uncontrollable. Whence many of the followers of the Mystery Schools were led away into both practical and technical error, so that writers of subsequent centuries were able to seize upon such lapses and magnify them into a general charge against those whom they regarded as heretics, completely ignoring the fact that the true students of the arcane sciences themselves were most emphatic in their condemnation of all such abuses.

c

THEURGY

One need hardly add that the explanations given to the Aspirant of the Mysteries dealt principally with the central object of all such schools, regeneration and rebirth, and not with generation, so that, accurately speaking, the conversion of the sacred symbols to this lower form of expression ought to be ignored from our present point of view, leaving us, therefore, only three real modes of interpreting them, which modes are, in the ultimate, one only.

We come thus to the most important aspect of our subject, the Serpent in relation to the upward path of the candidate in particular and of mankind in general. And this inevitably brings us into definite contact with our main subject, Spiritual Alchemy, Theurgy, the Therapeutics of the Soul and so forth, where all the symbols with which we have dealt will appear again, but invested with a new meaning as will be seen in the Chapter that follows.

CHAPTER IV

MAN, we are told, is the Microcosm or Little World, the Universe in Miniature, containing in himself the counterpart of all that is in the Great World or Macrocosm, whence the injunction " Gnothi Seauthon," " Know Thyself," inscribed over the portals of the Schools of the Mysteries.

We are also informed in the New Testament that man has three bodies, analogous to the three worlds, and more or less parallel with the three principal divisions of the soul according to the Qabalah and the Platonists. That is to say he possessed a spiritual, a psychic and a physical body, corresponding to the Archetypal, Psychic or Formative, and Material Worlds. These are also found in the Upanishads, where they are called the Causal, Subtile and Gross bodies, and their analogues may also be found in the Egyptian ideas on this subject.

The Causal, otherwise Spiritual, Pneumatic or Neshamah body, is really but ill-described as a body at all, for it is of the World of Briah, the Archangelic, Creative and truly formless World. From it, however, the other bodies may be considered as being derived,

35

and its manifestation to the eyes of the true seer—by which we do not mean the ordinary psychic or clairvoyant—would usually take the form of an oviform radiance or light, playing around the other, lower bodies, within which is the paraklete of the New Testament, which, in the symbolism which we are at present studying, is the Serpent, while the radiance or light is the ovum or egg. In the Greek this is called Speirema, the serpent coil, and in Sanskrit it is Kundalini, the annular force, which, in the Upanishads, is said to lie coiled up like a slumbering serpent. It is also the Dragon of the Alchemists and their internal fire.

So much nonsense has been written about Kundalini, relating it with physical sex currents, and indicating the most dangerous practices for arousing it, that we mention it with diffidence, at the same time reiterating the warning we gave in the previous Chapter.

This serpent is the good serpent, yet owing to the danger of it if quickened in the unpurified man, the Alchemists called it a poisonous dragon and many other kindred names, such as Typhon, Apophis, Firedrake, Satan, Aquafœtida, Ignis Gehennæ, Mortis Immundities, Venomous Black Toad and so forth, though this latter term is usually only used during the mortification.

The rousing of this force, and the preliminary preparations therefor, are said to be symbolised by

36

the Caduceus of Hermes, for the positive and negative currents represented by the two serpents must, it is alleged, be set in motion and equilibrated first before the Speirema can be stimulated, it being typified by the central rod. And this is further the Seed or Sperm or Ferment of the Alchemists, of the former of which it is said in the New Testament (1 Cor. xv. 36) " That which thou sowest is not quickened except it die." Unless it die, that is to say, to the material world of the senses, desires and passions, it cannot be truly quickened.

The symbol of the Spirit is Fire, which reappears here as the Serpent or Dragon, and elsewhere in Alchemy as one of their various Lions, Green, Red or Black according to the stage of the work. For in Astrology the sign Leo is the Kerubic Emblem of Fire, while the form of the sign is the glyph of a serpent, and the Hebrew Letter Teth, to which it is referred in the Sepher Yetzirah or Book of Formation (probably the oldest book of the Qabalah), means a serpent and is also a glyph of one. It is also well worth noting that the Speirema is a Solar Force, and that Leo is the Astrological House of the Sun.

Thomas Vaughan, dilating further upon the symbol of the Serpent placed diametrically across the circle, which we considered in the previous Chapter, explains that the Serpent is the Fiery nature, Alchemically Solar, which, of course, is Spirit—though he does not say this—while the wings, he adds, indicate the volatile, airy nature, which, as Ruach and Pneuma both mean breath, is also Spirit. " Lastly," he says, " the knot in the tail tells you this matter is of a most strong composition, and that the elements are fast bound in it."

Now all of this is rather similar to the example of scriptural exegesis regarding the Exodus, which we gave in the previous Chapter, for the word used for fiery serpents is Seraphim, and Moses was instructed to make the brazen serpent in the form of a Seraph, and to set it upon a pole, which, as we have already seen, was the central Pillar of the Sephiroth, the Pillar of Mildness or Equilibrium.

The name of this serpent, which, as we have previously stated, is Nogah, is also significant, for this is also the name of the Sphere of the Planet Venus, a fact which has confirmed many in their Phallic errors ; nevertheless a very small acquaintance with the literature dealing with that aspect of things will serve to demonstrate that its devotees see Phallic symbols everywhere. Mercifully in the great bulk of Alchemical writings we do not come across it, Venus, even in her most fiery aspect, bearing quite another significance.

The connection between the serpent and Venus, which we have noted above, is not uncommon among the allusions of the alchemists, a sample of it occurring, for example, in the third key of Eudoxus, where he says : " So in the Art you can have no success if you do not in the first work purify the Serpent, born of the Slime of the Earth; if you do not whiten these foul and black fœces, to separate from thence the white sulphur, which is the Sal Ammoniac of the Wise, and their Chaste Diana, who washes herself in the bath; and all this mystery is but the extraction of the fixed salt of our compound, in which the whole energy of our Mercury consists."

In the following passage from *Lumen de Lumine* by Thomas Vaughan, which is quite a good sample of Alchemical terminology, all these reappear, the twin serpents and the Dragon in his various metamorphoses; the fire, the love and the mind, or wisdom and understanding. He says:

"Take our two Serpents, which are to be found everywhere on the face of the earth. They are a living male and a living female. Tie them both in a love-knot and shut them up in the Arabian Caraha. This is thy first labour, but thy next is more difficult. Thou must encamp against them with the fire of Nature, and be sure thou dost draw thy line round about. Circle them in and stop all avenues, that they find no relief. Continue this siege patiently; and they will turn to an ugly, shabby, venomous, black toad, which will be transformed to a horrible, devouring Dragon—creeping and weltering in the bottom of her cave, without wings. Touch her not by any means, not so much as with thy hands, for there is not upon earth such a violent, transcendent poison. As thou hast begun, so proceed, and this Dragon will turn to a Swan, but more white than the hovering, virgin snow when it has not been sullied with the earth. Henceforth I will allow thee to fortify thy fire till the Phœnix appears. It is a red bird of a most deep colour with a shining, fiery hue. Feed this bird with the fire of his father and the ether of his mother; for the first is meat and the second is drink, and without this last he attains not to his full glory. Be sure to understand this secret, for fire feeds not well unless it first be fed. It is of itself dry and choleric; but a proper moisture tempers it, gives it a heavenly complexion and brings it to the desired exaltation. Feed thy bird then as I have told thee, and he will move in his nest and rise like a star in the firmament. Do this and thou hast placed Nature ' within the horizon of eternity.' Thou hast performed that command of the Qabalist: ' Unite the end to the beginning, like a flame to a coal; for God ' saith he, ' is superlatively one and He hath no second.' " (Sepher Yetzirah, Cap. i, sect. 7.) "Consider then what you seek: you seek an indissoluble, miraculous, transmuting, uniting union; but such a tie cannot be without the First Unity. ' To create,' saith one, ' and transmute essentially and naturally, or without any violence, is the only proper office of the First Power, the First Wisdom and the First Love.' Without this the elements will never be married; they will never

40

inwardly and essentially unite, which is the end and perfection of magic. Study then to understand this, and when thou hast performed I will allow thee that test of the Mekkubalim; 'Thou hast understood in wisdom, and thou hast been wise in understanding; thou hast established this subject upon the pure elements thereof, and thou hast posited the Creator on His throne.' " (Sepher Yetzirah, Cap. i, sect. 4.)

It is to be hoped that the above extract will not prove to be too disconcerting to the student, and we shall endeavour in subsequent Chapters to put forward one or two suggestions regarding the work that will, to some extent at least, throw light upon it. For the moment it will suffice to draw such parallels with what has gone before as may be seen between the toad and the passional nature; the dragon and the self-willed life; the cave, which, as the habitat of both these, is the body; and finally the star, into which the other natures are finally transmuted, rising above the limitations of the material.

Before passing on to the next stage of our inquiry, it would be as well to draw the attention to two versions of the same idea which we have already several times encountered, namely, the necessity for dying to the material world, and leaving the world of sense, for we shall have to revert to them later.

And lest anyone should be disappointed at such an apparently trite outcome of all that has gone before,

41

and retort " This much at least we knew in advance,"
we would reply that, as we shall hope to show later,
our meaning is to be taken not merely as indicating
the preliminaries, but also, in some measure, the means
to our end.

CHAPTER V

WE have now to begin to ask ourselves where all
this is leading us, and our answer is to be found
in a consideration of such records as have come down
to us of the schools or societies that were professedly
devoted to the study of the Sacred Mysteries.

For this purpose we may well take that historically
somewhat mysterious sect called the Therapeutæ.
Our main source of information concerning them is
the *De Vita Contemplativa* of Philo Judæus, but we
may glean a good deal of additional light on our subject
by comparing his statements with similar assertions by
writers representing other schools and cults.

We must remember that although Philo gives us
quite a good picture of the Wisdom Lovers, as he calls
them, allowance must be made for the fact that he
was but a lay brother, and, apart from any restrictions
imposed upon him, would have only a limited knowledge of the more recondite teachings of the fraternity
or of their practices.

As a preliminary we may take it that the Therapeuts
were not Christians, unless in the broad sense of
St. Augustine, who remarked that there never had been

but one religion since the world began, and that this commenced to be called Christian in Apostolic times. Nor can we assign to them any particular form of exoteric religion, despite Philo's attempt to claim that they were in the main Jews. On the contrary, it would appear probable that they were communities of Gnostic Ascetics, devoted to the Holy Life and Sacred Science.

Dealing with this point, G. R. S. Mead, in his *Fragments of a Faith Forgotten*, says : " Philo's . . . particular community . . . was mainly Jewish, though not orthodoxly so. . . . Others may have been tinged as strongly with Egyptian, Chaldean, Zoroastrian or Orphic elements. . . . It is further not incredible that there were truly eclectic communities among them who combined and synthesised the various traditions and initiations handed down by the doctrinally more exclusive communities, and it is in this direction, therefore, that we must look for light on the origins of Gnosticism, and for the occult background of Christianity. . . . I also think that . . . whatever works they may have put forward for or by lay-pupils were only a small part of their literature, and for those within there were those most highly mystical and abstruse treatises which none but the trained mystics could possibly understand."

Such a thesis is one with which we heartily agree, and a perusal of Philo's writings clearly indicates that
44

the non-eclectic communities tended to rely each upon the sacred writings of its own religion, knowing full well that all religions were but expressions of one, true, underlying religion, diversified only according to the various characteristics, racial and otherwise, of its propagators, but always couched in the same universal language of symbol and allegory. Each also knew that its scriptures were meant to be interpreted with understanding, and not to be treated merely as historical or even ethical.

Philo, of course, was a Jew, and appears to have been a lay brother of the Mareotic Jewish community south of Alexandria ; and it is interesting to note that, as we should have expected, they relied upon this interpretation of the scriptures. The term Qabalah, however, was not then in use, as the Oral Tradition had not at that time been committed to paper, as it has subsequently—though it is said that this is so only in part.

He tells us that " The Interpretation of the sacred scriptures is based upon certain undermeanings in the allegorical narratives ; for these men look upon the whole of their law-code as being like a living thing, having for body the spoken commands, and for soul the unseen thought stored up in the words (in which the rational soul begins to contemplate things native to its own nature more than anything else)—the interpretation, as it were, in the mirror of the names, catching sight of the extraordinary beauties of the ideas contained in them, and bringing to light the naked inner meanings."

Compare this with the following extracts from the Zohar III, fols. 149 and 152 (*La Kabbale*, Franck).

" If the Law was but composed of ordinary words and narratives, such as the words of Esau, of Hagar and of Laban, such as those uttered by Balaam's Ass and by Balaam himself, why should it be called the law of truth, the perfect law, and the faithful witness of God ? Why should the wise man value it as more precious than gold or than pearls ? But it is not so ; in each word of the Law is hidden a more recondite meaning : each narrative teaches us something other than the mere events that it appears to chronicle. And this superior Law is more Holy, it is the True Law."

" Woe to the man who sees in the Law but simple narratives and words ! For if in truth it contained but these, we should be able, even to-day, to compose for ourselves a law which should be even more worthy of admiration. For mere words we should but have to turn to the legislators of the world, among whom is often to be found somewhat of greater grandeur. It would suffice for us to compose a law in their style and words. But it is not thus. Each word of the Law contains a recondite and sublime mystery."

THEURGY

" The narratives of the Law are but the vestment of the Law. Woe unto him who takes the vestment for the Law itself! It is in this sense that David said : ' My God, open my eyes that I may see the marvels of Thy Law.' David spoke of that which is concealed beneath the vestment of the Law. There are those who are foolish enough, when they see a man clad in a beautiful garment, to look no further, nevertheless that which lends value to the garment is the body, and that which is still more precious is the soul. The Law has also its body. There are those commandments which may be called the body of the Law. The ordinary narratives which are intermingled there-with are the garments with which that body is clothed. The simple attend but to the outer garments or to the narratives of the Law ; they know nothing else ; they see not that which is concealed beneath the garment. The more instructed among men pay no attention to the garment, but only to the body which it covers. Finally the wise, the servants of the Supreme King, those who dwell upon the heights of Sinai, attend only to the soul, which is the basis of all the rest, which is the Law itself ; and in a time to come they will be prepared to contemplate the soul of this soul which breathes in the Law."

Dionysius (Epistle ix, Tito Episcopo.) says : " To know this is notwithstanding the crown of the work— that there is a two-fold tradition of the theologians, the one secret and mystical, the other evident and better known."

Again, the Church Father Origen on the same subject is worthy of note. In Homil. vii. in Levit., he says : " If it were necessary to lay emphasis on the letter of the Law and to understand what is written therein after the manner of the people, I should blush to say aloud that it is God Who has given us such Laws, and I should find more grandeur in human legislation, as for example in that of the Romans, Athenians or Lacedemonians." And in Homil. v. in Levit., he admits frankly the distinction between the historical moral and inner meanings, comparing them respectively to the body, soul and spirit.

Many more such statements could be quoted, but we must return to Philo, who intimates that the name Therapeutæ indicates " that they professed an art of healing superior to that used in the cities, for that only heals bodies, whereas this heals souls." Also, he adds, " Because they have been schooled by nature and the sacred laws to serve That which is better than the Good, and purer than the One and more ancient than the Monad."

This takes us to heights of sublimity where the mind finds it difficult to follow him, so let us see what light that great practical mystic, the author of the *Book of the Holy Hierotheos*, can throw on these ideas. This book, from which we take the extracts that follow, is presumed upon quite strong evidence to have been originally written by Proklos, who was initiated into the Mysteries, but to have been subsequently translated and overwritten by a Christian, who grafted upon it a Christian terminology and a large number of quotations from the Bible foreign to the original. Making due allowance, however, for these differences, it does not seem that the sense is in any way altered or the logical sequence of the book destroyed. Our author says :

" For when the Mind is accounted worthy of these things, it will not see by vision nor by form . . . for it is henceforth exalted in glorious and divine mystery to become above sight and form. . . . And henceforth it abandons even the name of Christ . . . and so neither loves nor desires to be brought near (the Father). . . . For lo, the very name of Love is a sign of distinction, for Love is not established by one but by two. . . . And then we will marvel at the mystery and say, ' O the depth and the riches and the wisdom and the intellect, far above the designation of God-head, of the Perfect Mind that has been fulfilled . . .' Let us then put away Unification and speak of Commingling . . . (for) the designation of Commingling is proper for Minds that have become ' above Unification. . . .' We cannot see the distinctions of Minds when they have Commingling with the Good . . . (for) Mind is no longer Mind when it is commingled. . . . Everything becomes One Thing ; for even God

D

shall pass, and Christ shall be done away, and the Spirit shall no more be called the Spirit. . . . This is the limit of All and the end of Everything. . . . All from One and One from All. . . . Before the first Beginning God was not God, and again, after the consummation of All He is not God."

Very similar is the fragment from the "Great Announcement" quoted by Hippolytus, and attributed by him to Simon Magus, translated as follows by G. R. S. Mead :

"To you, therefore, I say what I say, and write what I write. And the writing is this :

"Of the universal Aeons there are two growths, without beginning or end, springing from one Root, which is the Power Silence, invisible, inapprehensible. Of these one appears from above, which is the Great Power, the Universal Mind, ordering all things, male ; and the other, from below, the Great Thought (or conception), female, producing all things.

"Hence matching each other, they unite and manifest in the Middle Space, incomprehensible Air (Spirit) without beginning or end. In this (Air) is the (second) Father who sustains and nourishes all things which have beginning and end.

"This (Father) is He who has stood, stands and will stand, a male-female power, like the pre-existing Boundless Power, which has neither beginning nor end, existing in oneness. It was from this Boundless

Power that Thought, which had previously been hidden in oneness, first proceeded and became twain.

" He (the Boundless) was one ; having her in Himself, He was alone. Yet was He not ' first ' though ' pre-existing,' for it was only when He was manifested to Himself from Himself that there was a ' second.' Nor was He called Father before (Thought) called Him Father.

" As, therefore, producing Himself by Himself, He manifested to Himself His own Thought, so also His manifested Thought did not make the (manifested— the second) Father, but contemplating Him hid Him— that is, His power—in herself and is male-female, Power and Thought.

" Hence they match each other, being one ; for there is no difference between Power and Thought. From the things above is discovered Power, and from those below Thought.

" Thus it comes to pass that that which is manifested from them, though one, is found to be two, male-female, having the female in itself. Equally so is Mind in Thought ; they are really one, but when separated from each other they appear as two."

CHAPTER VI

BUT to return to our Therapeuts, Philo states that their aim was to arouse in themselves what he terms " that most indispensable of the senses. I mean not bodily sight, but that of the Soul, whereby truth and falsity are distinguished. . . . Let the race of Therapeutæ, being continually taught to see, aim at the vision of Reality, and pass by the Sun visible to sense."

In the attempt to attain to these heights they gave up all worldly possessions, and dwelt in communities, living in the simplest of dwellings. And in each dwelling, as Philo says, " is a sacred place called a shrine or monastery, in which in solitude they performed the mysteries of the holy life, whereby knowledge and devotion grow together and are perfected." He adds that at dawn and at even they were accustomed to offer up prayers, while the " whole interval from dawn to sunset they devote to their exercises."

We need hardly emphasise these two words " mysteries " and " exercises," which in the original are in sufficiently close proximity to attract one's attention, but this is a point with which we shall have to deal later.

THEURGY

Philo continues: "Taking the Sacred Writings, they spend their time in study, interpreting their ancestral code allegorically, for they think that the words of the literal meaning are symbols of a hidden nature, which is made plain only by the undermeaning." But with this point we have already dealt at sufficient length.

These and other such devotees carried on the tradition of the Mystery Schools of greater antiquity over against the Neo-Platonic teachings later inculcated by Plotinus and Porphyry, who taught a system analogous to the later Persian scheme, teaching that the Overmind, the Universal Soul and Nature proceeded by emanation from the Absolute One, and that to this Absolute there might be attained, for brief periods, by philosophic discipline, contemplation and ecstasy, as Wilder puts it, the gnosis or intimate union.

This is the great difference between Mysticism as such and the Theurgic or so-called Magical School, for the former was a system of impassiveness, and was discarded by the Hierophants, who laid it down that by practice of the Theurgic Rites the Soul exalts itself over the Over-Mind and becomes at one with the Absolute, that it can even become permanently at one.

Of these practices Iamblichos says in his *De Mysteriis:* " It is not the concept that unites the theurgic priests to the Gods ; else what is there to hinder those who pursue philosophic speculation contemplatively from

53

having theurgic union to the Gods? Now . . . this is not the case. . . . It is the complete fulfilling of the Arcane performances, the carrying of them through in a manner worthy of the Gods and surpassing all conception, and likewise the power of the voiceless symbols which are perceived by the Gods alone, that establishes the Theurgic Union. Hence we do not effect these things by thinking."

We have previously quoted Clemens Alexandrinus, one of the most celebrated of the Fathers of the early Church. The first three books of his lost work, *The Outlines*, bear a strong resemblance to the three stages of the Platonists—Purification, Initiation and Direct Vision, or, as Iamblichos classifies them, Coming to the Divinity, Assimilation into the likeness of the Divinity and Perfection.

This latter authority, speaking of what the invocations accomplish, tells us that " By such a purpose, therefore, the Gods being gracious and propitious, give forth light abundantly to the Theurgists, both calling their souls upward into themselves . . . and accustoming them while they are yet in the body, to hold themselves aloof from corporeal things, and likewise to be led up to their own eternal and noetic First Cause. . . . From these performances . . . the soul reciprocates another life, is linked with another energy, and rightly reviewing the matter, it seems to be not even a human energy, but the most blessed energy of

the Gods. . . . The upward way through the invocations effects for the priests a purifying of the
passions, a release from the conditions of generated
life and likewise a union to the Divine Cause. . . .
(They) by no means, as the term seems to imply,
(involve) an inclining of the mind of the Gods to
human beings, but on the contrary, as the truth itself
will teach, the adapting of the human intelligence to
the participating of the Gods, leading it upward to
them and bringing it into accord. . . . (So that) the
Rites performed by the Adepts in superior knowledge
bring them to the superior races, and attach them
together by becoming assimilated."

And this leads to the beholding or epopteia in its
highest sense, of which Hierotheos says that " To the
Pure Mind belongs the power of seeing above and
below . . . for the full account of the secret of the
Pure Mind (is) without limit and embraces everything." And he adds that he is speaking of things
that he has seen.

At this point, perhaps, it should be made clear that
when we speak of Gods, as we have done and shall do
still further, especially in quotations, it should not be
thought that we are getting away from the fundamental
idea of an essential monotheism. Nor was any such
idea in the minds of the leaders of the Mysteries,
whether in Egypt or elsewhere. The term Gods or
Divinities was a technical term denoting certain high

orders of Spiritual Beings, who, as compared with us, were best described as Gods. Such were, for example, the Gnostic Aeons, the Elohim of Genesis, some of the Greek Daimones, many of the Egyptian Deities and so forth.

Before all these; before manifestation; before the things that really are; before even the first principles of all things; prior to the Good; prior to the One; prior even to Being or Thinking, there is That which is shut out from all mortal comprehension.

As the ancient Oracle said: " In Him is an illimitable abyss of glory, and from it there goeth forth one little spark, which maketh all the glory of the Sun and of the Moon and of the Stars. Mortal, behold how little I know of God; seek not to know more of Him, for this is far beyond thy comprehension, however wise thou art; as for us, who are His ministers, how small a part are we of Him ! "

But to resume. Everywhere, so far, we have been met by the idea of Rites and Ceremonies, Exercises, Magic and so forth, and it would perhaps be as well to examine a little more carefully what these people meant by Magic. In the minds of many it is associated with the Grimoires and such-like literature; with Necromancy and other unpleasant arts, such as the making of wax images and sticking pins in them and so forth. It is, however, on the contrary, claimed by the Theurgists that it is the Wisdom and Philosophy of Nature and a

perfect knowledge of the works of God and their
effects. A Magus is therefore a Contemplator of
Heavenly and Divine things ; a wise man and a priest,
who, to paraphrase Picus di Mirandola, by the connection of natural agents and patients, answerable each
to the other, may bring forth such effects as are wonderful to those that know not their causes.

Paracelsus, in his *Occult Philosophy*, Cap. II, says :
" It is a most secret and hidden Science of supernatural
things in the Earth, that whatsoever is impossible to be
found out by man's reason may by this Art, that is
most pure and not defiled." While Cornelius Agrippa,
who also wrote three books on Occult Philosophy, says
(Book I, Cap. 2) : " Magic contains the profoundest
contemplation of the most secret things, together with
the nature, power, quality, substance and virtues thereof, as also the knowledge of whole nature."

Elias Ashmole, who published the *Theatrum Chemi-
cum Britannicum* (1652), summarises the position in his
notes to Norton's *Ordinall of Alchimy*, by saying:
" The Magic here intended is Divine, True, of the
wisdom of nature, and indeed comprehendeth the
whole Philosophy of Nature, being a perfect knowledge
of the works of God and their effects. It is that which
reduces all natural philosophy from variety of speculation to the magnitude of works, and whose mysteries
are far greater than all natural philosophy now in use
and reputation will reach unto." Which statement,

we are of opinion—without wishing to offend—is as true to-day as the day it was made.

This involves the theory of Agrippa that the order and symmetry of the Universe is so regulated that the lowest things, belonging to the sub-celestial or elementary region are immediately subservient to the middle or celestial, and these in turn to the super-celestial or intelligible, while these last obey the Supreme. That further there is an analogical bond between them by which the spiritual essences may be drawn down, or, rather, a particular spirit may be united to the Universal, the simple and pure human mind being converted and laid asleep from its present life so utterly as to be brought into its divine nature and become enlightened with the divine light.

And this is in harmony with the Egyptian Theurgists, who said that the Gods were Spiritual Essences, and were partaken of as light, leaving the light unaffected, while the partaker was filled, receiving every excellent quality of mind, being purified and set free from all passions and irregular impulses. To the quest of this light it was necessary that everyone should give himself wholly, for by its means is obtained both truth and perfect excellence in souls, by the aid of both of which the Theurgist winged his way upwards to the Intellectual Fire which is the end of all knowledge and of all Theurgic practice.

This is the Fire spoken of by the Oracle. " And

when, after all the phantoms, thou shalt see that Holy and Formless Fire; that Fire that darts and flashes through the hidden depths of the Universe, hear thou the Voice of Fire."

But the Oracle also says, " So therefore, first the Priest who governeth the works of Fire, must sprinkle with the Water of the loud-resounding Sea." So that the first preliminary must be purification, without which nothing may be attempted of a more profound order, for according to another saying of the same Oracle : " Thou shalt not invoke the self-conspicuous Image of Nature, ere thy body has been purged by the Sacred Rites, since ever seeking to drag down the Soul, from the confines of matter leap forth the terrestrial demons, showing no true sign unto mortal man."

CHAPTER VII

THIS magic, therefore, these rites, ceremonies and exercises, were in the first stages directed to a purging and purification of the lower nature, uniting it thereafter to its various higher counterparts until, having gathered itself together, as it were, having achieved a state of unification of itself, it might attempt the supreme and final operation of at-one-ment or commingling, uniting itself indissolubly with that which is beyond all idea of selfhood. But this latter stage is entirely removed from all human comprehension, even the preceding stage taking place, as we are not surprised to learn, at a very late period, and then only with the exceeding few.

But we are plainly told that there is " but one linear way throughout " from the purifications upwards, so that we may well make our start here, nearer to earth.

We may, of course, take it as a *sine qua non* that the aspirant must lead a life as far as possible virtuous and unselfish, but this is merely a necessary condition, for without some assistance the mere abstaining from evil is sufficiently difficult and far from being all that is required. The very desire to do evil must cease to exist ; temptations must cease to be temptations if we are to achieve our end. And this is not to be attained by the stern repression of all emotions and feelings, the " rooting out " that is so much spoken of and so much mistaken ; for the emotions are the driving force, without which nothing can be accomplished, and the destruction of them is not for one moment to be contemplated.

Transmutation is what is required, and here we should note that as Friar Bacon—and with him all the others agree—tells us, " Species are not transmuted, but their subject matter rather, therefore the first work is to reduce the body into water, that is into mercury, and this is called Solution, which is the foundation of the whole art."

This is so plain and definite a statement, and one that is so often expressed by all the authorities in almost identical terms, that we cannot afford to overlook it, and it would be as well, therefore, to try and ascertain what was meant by this before endeavouring to discover any clue to how it was to be done.

In the *Triumphal Chariot of Antimony*, Basil Valentine, dealing with the necessity for depriving Antimony of its poisonous nature so that it can never return to it, throws considerable light on the subject. To avoid undue prolixity we shall quote principally from the somewhat abridged translation of A. E. Waite, condensing even this so as to present essentials only.

And lest his illustration appear to be too " rustic "—
to use his own terms—we will first give the reader the
remarks of his commentator, Kirchringius, on the
passage in question. He says :

" This first key is the principal part of the whole
Art ; this opens the first gate, this will also unlock the
last, which leads into the palace of the king. Believe
not only, but consider and observe. Here you stand in
the entrance ; if you miss the door, all your course
will be error ; all your haste ruin ; and all your wisdom
foolishness. He who obtains this key, and knows the
method by which to use it, and hath strength to turn
the same, will acquire riches, and an open passage into
the mysteries of alchemy. Do not despise these remarks.
There may be apparent repetition here, but there is
nothing superfluous. Return often mentally to them ;
read, mark, learn and inwardly digest all that is said.
It may be that in this turbid water, which looks so
unlikely, you may after all catch your fish. If the
excess of light which prevails here should not enable
you to see, no amount of obscure alchemistic reading
will disperse your inward darkness."

This is at least encouraging. It is to be hoped that
the reader will not find the remarks of Valentine himself the reverse. He says : " Here lies the master key
of our whole Art. Antimony, which contains within
itself its own vinegar, should be so prepared as to entirely
remove its poisonous nature. The preparation of

THEURGY

Antimony or the Key of Antimony, is that by which it is dissolved, opened, divided and separated. In extracting its essence, in vitalizing its Mercury, the process is continued and this Mercury must afterwards be precipitated in the form of a fixed powder.

" The same process may be observed for instance in the brewing of beer ; barley, wheat or other grain must undergo all these processes before it becomes a palatable beverage. It must first be mashed and dissolved in water. This is Putrefaction or Corruption. Then the water is poured off and the moist grain is left in a warm place till it germinates and sticks together. This is Digestion. Thereupon the grains are once more separated from each other, and dried, either in the sun or before the fire. This is Reverberation or Coagulation.

" The prepared germ is then ground in the mill. This is vegetable calcination. It is afterwards cooked over the fire, and its nobler spirit is mingled with the water in a way which would not have been possible before it was so prepared. This we may call distillation. This method of converting water into a fermented beverage by the extraction of the spirit of the grain is unknown to (many and) I have only found a few who understand such Art.

" Afterwards a new separation takes place by means of Clarification. A little yeast is added, which stirs up its internal heat and motion, and thus in time the gross is separated from the subtle and the pure from the impure. The beer thereby becomes of great efficacy ; before this clarification this would not be because such operative spirit was clogged and hindered by its own uncleanness from fulfilling its objects.

" After this we may bring about another separation by means of Vegetable Sublimation. The spirit, by this process, and by Distillation, is separated in the form of another beverage, or ardent spirits. Here the operative virtue is separated from its body ; the spirit is extracted by means of fire, and has deserted its inert and lifeless habitation in which before it was domiciled.

" If such ardent spirit be rectified, you have Exaltation. When this is done and the spirit is several times distilled, it becomes, by being purified from all phlegm and wateriness, twenty times more effective than before, and is volatile and subtle and penetrating.

" Know that these illustrations set forth a grand truth of the highest moment, which I have set forth lest you might be in danger of losing your route at the very outset. (For) Antimony is also likened to a bird which is borne through the air on the wings of the wind, and turns whither it will. The wind or the air here represents the Artist, who can move and impel Antimony whither it pleases him, and place it wherever he likes."

At the end of the *Triumphal Chariot* in the section on the " Fire Stone " he gives us a brief but

64

plain statement regarding this solution or separation, which causes his commentator, Kirchringius, to exclaim : " Are you in your right mind, Basilius, so to prostitute the Stone, which has hitherto been so carefully kept a secret by all the Sages ? You have here let out the whole secret."

The reader may not exactly share Kirchringius' anxiety—though we cannot but hope that he will—nevertheless here is what Valentine says : " But no substance can be of any use in the generation of our Stone without fermentation. From the tangible and formal body we must elicit the spiritual and celestial entity (I hardly know what expression to use in describing it). But to what purpose do I speak, and what do I say ? I speak as one who has temporarily lost control over his organs of speech. If an atom of judgment still remained to me, I should not have opened my mouth so wide, and I should have stayed my hand even at the last moment."

Equally to the point is Lucas in the sixty-seventh Dictum of the *Turba Philosophorum* when he says : " I testify that the definition of this Art is the liquefaction of the body and the separation of the soul from the body which it penetrates." And Synesius, when he tells us that " The Quintessence is none other than our viscous, celestial and glorious soul, drawn from its minera by our magistery."

If we might ourselves offer any commentary, we

would say that the secret is safe enough as far as the vast majority is concerned, for though something may be tolerably obvious by now of what has to be done in this first part of the work, yet it is only, as it were, the first half of the first part, and that without any details and without any clue as to how this separation is to be brought about.

The first omission may easily be rectified, for everywhere in the literature of this subject we encounter variants on the ancient theme " Solve et Coagula," dissolve and coagulate, volatilise and fix. And these two are but complementary portions of one operation, and are therefore frequently treated of as being one. Indeed, at least in Spiritual Alchemy, the great variety of terms we encounter, such as reverberation, circulation, cohobation, mollification, decension, putrefaction, etc., is merely a repetition of these two processes separately or combined.

This we may see from that saying of the Philosophers quoted by Solomon Trismosin, the reputed teacher of Paracelsus, in his *Splendor Solis*, where he says in his second treatise, " Dissolve the thing and sublimate it, and then distil it, coagulate it, make it ascend, make it descend, soak it, dry it, and ever up to an indefinite number of operations, all of which take place at the same time and in the same vessel."

Compare this with Albertus Magnus, who says : " Take the occult nature, which is our Brass, and

66

wash it that it may be pure and clean ; dissolve, distil, sublime, incerate, calcine and fix it ; the whole of which is nothing else than a successive dissolution and coagulation to make the fixed volatile and the volatile fixed. The beginning of the whole work is a perfect solution." And Synesius, who takes us at the same time a stage further in his description, saying : " Note that to dissolve, to calcine, to tinge, to whiten, to renew, to bathe, to wash, to coagulate, to imbibe, to decoct, to fix, to grind, to dry, and to distil are all one and signify no more than to decoct nature until such time as she be perfected. Note further that to extract the soul or the spirit . . . is nothing else than the aforesaid calcinations. . . . It is through the fire of the extraction of the soul that the spirit comes forth gently ; understand me, the same may be said of the extraction of the soul out of the body, and the reduction of it afterwards upon the same body until . . . that which is below, being like unto that which is above, there are made manifest two luminaries, the one fixed, the other not . . . (And when ultimately) that which is below rises upon that which is above (then) all being substantiated, there issues forth an incomparable Luminary."

We may therefore, it would seem, conclude this part of our investigation by thus amplifying the deduction made at the end of our fourth chapter. Not merely have we to purify as far as possible the human spirit, but to make an extraction of it, so that it may, in a measure, literally leave the world of sense, and become that flying volatile of which Hermes speaks. After which we must bring it again into its body, which is to be tinged thereby. But the general consensus of opinion among our authors is that this cannot be in any way effected without prayer, so that it would be as well to see what they have to tell us regarding this before proceeding further.

CHAPTER VIII

FROM the very outset, then, we are to regard prayer, with which we include the proper use of invocations, ceremonial and ritual where necessary, as not the least important part of the sacred rites, both purificatory and telestic. And the Alchemists tell us, no less than the Hierophants of the Mysteries, the Prophets of the Old Testament and the Apostles of the New, that without it nothing may be accomplished.

Norton, in the first Chapter of his Ordinal, says :

> " Maistryefull merveylous and Archimastrye
> Is the tincture of holi Alkimy :
> A wonderful Science, secrete Philosophie,
> A singular grace & gifte of th' almightie ;
> Which never was founde by labour of Mann,
> But it by Teaching, or Revelation begann.
> It was never for Mony sold ne bought,
> By any Man which for it sought :
> But given to an able man by grace,
> Wrought with great Cost, with long laysir and space.
> Also no man coulde yet this Science reach,
> But if God send a Master him to teach :
> For it is soe wonderfull and soe selcouth,
> That it must needes be tought from mouth to mouth.
> For God's Conjunctions Man maie not undoe,
> But if his Grace fully consent thereto,
> By helpe of this Science, which our Lord above
> Hath given to such Men as he doth love :
> Wherefore old Fathers conveniently
> Called this Science Holy Alkimy,"

And Hermes, in the *Tractatus Aureus*, declares that
" This science and art I have obtained by the inspiration of the living God alone, who judged fit to open
them to me His servant." While Zachary, in the
Opusculum, is equally definite. " For no one," he
says, " ever acquired this art by chance, but by prayer
rather than by any other means."

Basil Valentine calls this prayer the Invocation of
God, and his commentator Kirchringius gives us some
analyses of it, which we may with profit scrutinise.
" Every man knows," he says, " that hath entirely
devoted himself to this business, how effectual prayer
is, and how often those things which he long sought
and could not find, have been imparted to him in a
moment, as it were, infused from above or dictated by
some good genius. That is also of use in solving
riddles and enigmatical writings ; for if you burn
with a great desire of knowing them, that is prayer :
and when you incline your mind to this or that,
variously discussing and meditating many things, this
is co-operation : that your prayer may not be, for want
of exertion, a tempting of God ; yet all endeavour
is vain until you find a solution. Nevertheless, if you
despair not, but instantly persist in desire, and cease
not from labour, at length, in a moment, the solution
will fall in ; this is revelation, which you cannot receive
unless you pray with great desire and labour, using
your utmost endeavour ; and yet you cannot perceive

70

how from all those things of which you thought, which were not the solution of the enigma, the solution itself arose. This unfolding of the Riddle opens to you the mystery of all things, and shows how available prayer is for the obtainment of things spiritual and eternal as well as corporeal and perishing good : and when prayer is made with a heart not feigned, but sincere, you will see that there is nothing more fit for the acquiring of what you desire."

But prayer must not be considered, in the invocations of the mysteries, or in one's private meditations, as being used with any deluded notion of influencing the Gods and changing their minds, as if they were vacillating entities like ourselves, subject to flattery and capable of being swayed by a petition adroitly addressed. Nor should anyone suppose that the purpose of the Rituals and Formulæ is to force the Gods to this or that manifestation of their powers, as if man should set himself up to be higher than they, for indeed it is far otherwise.

But there is an essential something in us that is divine, or mental essence if this term be preferred, something at least that is or can be vividly aroused in and by prayers ; and this, when fully aroused, longs ardently and strenuously for its counterpart, and becomes united to the absolute perfection, though this latter consummation is not to be understood as an immediate result, but rather as the outcome of prolonged and concentrated endeavour.

It may be argued that it is not necessary to pray to God or to the Gods, as pure mental or spiritual essences would require neither praise nor adulation, which could be addressed properly only to God made in man's image, and that prayers for material needs should not be made, on the ground that what is good for us will be given, and that what we want is known before we ask it. But this is a mistaking of the whole rationale of prayer, which is, at least to a great extent, that the very act of praying benefits us in and of itself, and not because it is heard or received through any sense-faculty.

For if we judge ourselves honestly and fairly, comparing ourselves with the Gods, then the very consciousness of our own nothingness leads us to a form of supplication of, or meditation on, the Divine nature, so that, as Iamblichos puts it, " We are led from supplication to the object of supplication, and from the familiar intercourse we acquire a similarity to it, and from imperfection we quietly receive the Divine Perfection." And if there is any relationship, however remote, between our meditation and the reality, it will serve as a bond or link to draw us nearer to our source, " For there is not anything which is in the least degree akin to the Gods with which the Gods are not immediately present and conjoined."

THEURGY

There are thus three main types of prayer, the first of which involves a collecting and concentrating of our thoughts, which of itself will lead gradually to a contact with and genuine knowledge of God. Next comes that which effects the " binding in communion with a single mind." Lastly, in the most perfect form of prayer, the degree of elevation is such that the mysterious union is sealed and its validity assured.

The first of these, as Iamblichos says, relates to illumination, the second to a general completion of effort, and the third to complete fulfilment by means of the Fire or Supreme Deity.

These stages are parallel with those enumerated by Proklos, which are the contact, the approach and the perfect union. They are preceded by the knowledge of the different ranks of the divine beings to which they belong, and the bond of union by which we become adopted by the Gods.

It may be as well, in view of the way in which this branch of our subject is usually misunderstood, to say something about the so-called " propitiations of anger," for when we understand what view the Theurgists took of the anger of the Gods, the matter is plain enough. Far from regarding it from the apparently obvious standpoint, they held that, as far as it related to the Gods, it was a turning away on our part from their beneficence, much as if we were deliberately to cut ourselves off from the sunlight by shutting ourselves away in the dark. The object of the " propitiation," therefore, was to turn ourselves back to the participation of the supernal natures, to lead us once more to the enjoyment of the communion we had interrupted and once more to bind harmoniously together both those participating and the essences participated.

Thus we learn that prayers are an integral and indispensable part of the Sacred Rites of the Mysteries, and that continual exercise in them nourishes the mind, as it were, and renders what has been termed the receptivity of the soul more spacious. At the same time it accustoms us to the irradiations of that Light towards which we are striving, and by degrees makes clear the arcane knowledge of the Supernal Wisdom, gradually but steadily drawing the sublimated soul to the very summit of all possible progress.

To be brief then, and at the risk of seeming to be redundant, just as prayer is not supposed to influence or change the minds of the Gods, but rather to effect a somewhat in us that brings us into contact with the Higher Powers, so also the Invocations were not assumed to have any compelling force upon the Divinities, but to turn us towards the participation of the superior nature and to create a binding link between those participating and the essences participated.

On which point Proklos is clear when he says : " In the invocations and at the Autopsia, the Divine

Essence seems after a manner to come down to us, when we are really extending ourselves to it instead."

It may appear to some that we have dealt with this whole section at undue length, but in our opinion this is not so, for we hold it to be of considerable importance in the work. In conclusion, however, we should perhaps make it clear that prayer does not of necessity involve at all times the use of verbal expression, or the direction of the prayer to a personal entity. Both these types are a stumbling-block to many, and we do not find that they are as a rule insisted upon by the majority of our authorities. But there are other, wordless methods, meditation, aspiration and the like that should be practised, " For if," says Vaughan in his *Coelum Terrae*, " thy desire leads thee on to the practice, consider well what manner of man thou art, and what it is that thou wouldst do ; for it is no small matter. Thou hast resolved with thyself to be a co-operator with the living God, and to minister to Him in His work of generation. Have a care, therefore, that thou dost not hinder His work." " Settle not in the lees and puddles of the world " ; he says also in his *Anima Magia Abscondita*, " have thy heart in heaven and thy hands upon the earth. Ascend in piety and descend in charity. For this is the Nature of Light and the way of the children of it."

CHAPTER IX

WE now come to the most difficult part of our inquiry, for we are beginning to grasp the magnitude of the task that we propose for ourselves, which is nothing less than the purification of the spiritual nature to a point where it may be raised, exalted or sublimated to a real union with its higher counterparts ; from which mystical marriage, as it is sometimes called, is born that which is more than human, that which may be termed divine, the risen Osiris or Christ, which is truly at one with the Eternal Gods, with True Being.

And such an undertaking involves an ascent from World to World by analogous processes in each, by becoming perfect in each. Step by step we must climb that Jacob's ladder which stretches from earth to the super-celestial regions, purifying and purging at every stage, dissolving, distilling, calcining, imbibing, coagulating, subliming, until the goal is reached, a goal so far beyond our most vivid imaginative speculations that all attempts fail of describing.

For, as Porphyry tells us in his *Auxiliary to the Perception of Intelligibles*, " When you have assumed to yourself an Eternal Essence, infinite in itself according to power; and begin to perceive intellectually an hypostasis unwearied, untamed, and never failing, but transcending in the most pure and genuine life, and full from itself; and which likewise, is established in itself; to this essence, if you add a subsistence in place, or a relation to a certain thing, at the same time you diminish this essence, or rather appear to diminish it, by ascribing to it an indigence of place or a relative condition of being; you do not, however, in reality diminish this essence, but you separate yourself from the perception of it, by receiving as a veil the phantasy which runs under your conjectural apprehension of it. For you cannot pass beyond, or stop, or render more perfect, or effect the least change in a thing of this kind, because it is impossible for it to be in the smallest degree deficient. For it is much more sufficient than any perpetually flowing fountain can be conceived to be. If, however, you are unable to keep pace with it, and to become assimilated to the whole Intelligible Nature, you should not investigate anything pertaining to real Being; or if you do, you will deviate from the path that leads to it, and will look at something else; but if you investigate nothing else, being established in yourself and in your own Essence, you will be assimilated to the Intelligible Universe, and will not adhere to anything posterior to it.

" Neither therefore should you say, I am of great

77

magnitude ; for omitting this idea of greatness, you will become universal, as you were universal prior to this. But when, together with the universe, something was present with you, you became less by the addition ; because the addition was not from truly subsisting Being, for to that you cannot add anything. When, therefore, anything is added from the subjective self-hood, a place is afforded to poverty as an associate, accompanied by an indigence of all things. Hence, dismissing non-being (the subjective self-hood) you will then become sufficient ; for when anyone is present in himself, then he is present with true Being, which is everywhere ; but when you withdraw from yourself, then likewise you recede from real Being ; of such great consequence is it for a man to be present with that which is present with himself, that is to say, with his rational part, and to be absent from that which is external to him."

It must be our present purpose, therefore, having sketched briefly the objects proposed, and emphasised the seriousness of the undertaking, to attempt some investigation of the methods by which these ends may be attained, the *modus operandi* of the Hermetic Practice.

This is usually divided into two parts, termed the Gross and the Subtle, but as Morien says : "You shall know that the whole work of this Art ends in two Operations hanging very close together, so that when one is complete, the other may begin and finish, this perfecting the whole Magistery."

An analysis of the works of the Philosophers shows that these two operations are again sub-divided, broadly speaking, into two for the first and three for the second, though these are themselves each multiple and are infinitely varied by the different authorities, who complicate matters still further by frequent introversions of the order of the work, scattering their instructions apparently at random through their books, as they themselves freely confess, in order that they may not be too apparent to the uninitiated.

These five principal divisions of the process may be tabulated as Preparation, Solution, Conversion, Separation, Reunion; though it must be remembered that each stage includes operations similar to what has gone before, recapitulations, repetitions and so forth, so that our classification is in no wise as simple as it appears.

Before proceeding to any attempt at analysing them, we would like to place before the reader a quotation from the *Azoth* of M. Georgius Beatus, who was, as we are informed by Vaughan in his *Coelum Terrae*— though he does not mention his name—one of the Fratres R.C. This extract sets forth more clearly than many the whole matter, though we are bound to admit that his meaning will in many places be more apparent to the student who has already some familiarity with the Holy Qabalah. Nevertheless, an intelligent

79

comparison with what we have set forth in the preceding chapters should serve to elucidate the majority of his points, while what we have yet to say will be of service, we hope, in considering the remainder. He says :

" I am a goddess for beauty and extraction famous, born out of our proper sea which compasseth the whole earth and is ever restless. Out of my breasts I pour forth milk and blood : boil these two till they are turned into silver and gold. O most excellent subject, out of which all things in this world are generated, though at first sight thou art poison, adorned with the name of the Flying Eagle. Thou art the First Matter, the seed of Divine Benediction, in whose body there is heat and rain, which notwithstanding are hidden from the wicked, because of thy habit and virgin vestures, which are scattered over all the world. Thy parents are the sun and moon ; in thee there is water and wine, gold also and silver upon earth, that mortal man may rejoice. After this manner God sends us His blessing and wisdom and rain, and the beams of the sun, to the eternal glory of His name.

" But consider, O man, what things God bestows upon thee by thus means. Torture the Eagle till she weeps and the Lion be weakened and bleed to death. The blood of this Lion incorporated with the tears of the Eagle is the treasure of the earth. These creatures use to devour and kill one another, but notwithstanding their love is mutual, and they put on the property and nature of a Salamander, which if it remains in the fire without any detriment, it cures all the diseases of men, beasts and metals.

"After that the ancient philosophers had perfectly understood this subject, they diligently sought in this mystery for the centre of the middlemost tree in the Terrestrial Paradise, entering in by five litigious gates. The first gate was the knowledge of the True Matter, and here arose the first and that a most bitter conflict. The second was the preparation by which this Matter was to be prepared, that they might obtain the embers of the Eagle and the blood of the Lion. At this gate there was a most sharp fight, for it produceth water and blood and a spiritual, bright body. The third gate is the fire, which conduceth to the maturity of the Medicine. The fourth gate is that of multiplication and augmentation, in which proportions and weight are necessary. The fifth and last gate is projection. But most glorious, full rich and high is he who attains to the fourth gate, for he hath got an universal Medicine for all diseases. This is that great character of the Book of Nature out of which her whole alphabet doth arise. The fifth gate serves only for metals.

"This mystery, existing from the foundation of the world and the creation of Adam, is of all others the most ancient, a knowledge which God Almighty—

by His Word—breathed into Nature, a miraculous
power, the blessed fire of life, the transparent carbuncle
and red gold of the wise men, and the Divine Benediction of this life. But this mystery, because of the
wickedness of men, is given only to few, notwithstanding
it lives and moves every day in the sight of the whole
world, as it appears by the following parable.

" I am a poisonous dragon, present everywhere and
to be had for nothing. My water and my fire dissolve
and compound. Out of my body thou shalt draw the
Green and Red Lion; but if thou dost not exactly
know me thou wilt—with my fire—destroy thy five
senses. A most pernicious, quick poison comes out of
my nostrils which hath been the destruction of many.
Separate therefore the thick from the thin artificially,
unless thou dost delight in extreme poverty. I give
thee faculties both male and female and the powers
both of heaven and earth. The mysteries of my art
are to be performed magnanimously and with great
courage, if thou wouldst have me overcome the
violence of the fire, in which attempt many have
lost both their labour and their substance. I am the
egg of Nature, known only to the wise, such as are
pious and modest, who make of me a little world.
Ordained I was by the Almighty God for men, that
they may relieve the poor with my treasures and not
set their minds on gold that perisheth. I am called
the Philosophers' Mercury; my husband is gold

philosophical. I am the old dragon that is present everywhere on the face of the earth. I am father and mother, youthful and ancient, weak and yet most strong, life and death, visible and invisible, hard and soft, descending to the earth and ascending to the heavens, most high and most low, light and heavy. In me the order of nature is oftentimes inverted—in colour, number, weight and measure. I have in me the light of Nature; I am dark and bright; I spring from the earth and I come out of heaven; I am well known and yet mere nothing; all colours shine in me and all metals by the beams of the sun. I am the Carbuncle of the Sun, a most noble, clarified earth, by which thou mayest turn copper, iron, tin and lead into most pure gold."

Let us, however, now proceed to our investigation of the various stages of the work. Firstly we have the preparation, which, as we have sufficiently indicated, involves as careful and thorough a purification of the whole nature as a constantly directed will, aided by prayer, meditation and aspiration can bring about. To this must be added systematic study to know the Matter, to understand what it is with which we are to deal, and to an elucidation of this we have devoted the greater part of what has gone before.

But to recapitulate, we may say with Synesius, as in Chapter VII, " that the Quintessence is none other than our viscous, celestial and glorious soul, drawn from

its minera by our magistery." And with Paracelsus that
" that which we see is only the receptacle; the true
element is a spirit of life that grows in all things, as
the soul in the body of man. This is the First Matter
of the elements, which can neither be seen nor felt,
and yet is in all things. And the First Matter of the
elements is nothing else than the life that the creatures
have; and it is these magical elements which are of
such an excellent and quick activity that nothing
besides can be found or imagined like them."

But even these pre-requisites do not suffice, for a
knowledge of the matter must be supplemented by a
knowledge of the elements—that is theoretically, for
at this stage we have not advanced to any really
practical experimentation such as will lead to first-hand
knowledge. But when the philosophers speak of a
knowledge of the elements, they do not mean
corporeally, but spiritually and wisely, " non corpor-
aliter, sed spiritualiter et sapienter."

Then, again, some study of cosmogony and cosmology
must be undertaken, for without this, seeing that man
is but the microcosm, it is not possible for him safely
to obtain sufficient knowledge of himself to proceed to
subsequent stages except by practising an amount of
introspection that is dangerous.

We shall also see later on a further necessity for this
latter class of knowledge, apart from the value of it in
teaching the aspirant self-understanding by means of

the parallels between the macrocosmic universe and himself.

All these are indispensable, and without them no one is advised to apply himself to this work, else, as we are plainly told, he will lose his labour and stray far from the true path. Let the aspirant to the mastery of the Alchemic Art, therefore, pledge himself from the very start to a life of stern endeavour and rigid application.

CHAPTER X

WE now come to the second part of the first or Gross Work, which is Solution, and a study of the Alchemical writers will soon assure us that this is the most important part of the work, and the key to all the rest.

Here, also, more have erred than in any other part, and it is well said " Qui scit Salem et ejus solutionem, scit secretum occultum antiquorum philosophorum," Who knows the Salt and its solution, knows the hidden secret of the Ancient Sages.

" Here lies the knot," says Vaughan, " and who is he that will untie it ? " In reply to which we may quote Raymond Lully, who tells us that it was never put to paper " Because it is the office of God only to reveal this thing, and man seeks to take away from the Divine Glory when he publishes, by word of mouth or in writing, what appertains to God alone. Therefore thou canst not attain this operation until thou hast first been approved spiritually for the favours of Divinity. For this secret is of no human revelation, but for that Benign Spirit Which breathes where it wills."

86

THEURGY

Despite this somewhat damping information, there is yet much that we can do, for we can at least discover, from a careful perusal of their instructions, what the solution is, and we should therefore not be unduly discouraged, for this is undoubtedly a step towards ascertaining how it might be done.

Eudoxus, in his second Key, gives us an inkling as to what it is, giving us hints how to find out the secret, encouraging us to believe that we can do so. " The Second Key," he says, " dissolves the compound of the Stone and begins the separation of the Elements in a philosophical manner : this separation of the elements is not made but by raising up the subtle and pure parts above the thick and terrestrial parts. He who knows how to sublime the Stone philosophically, justly deserves the name of a philosopher, since he knows the Fire of the Wise, which is the only Instrument which can work this sublimation. No philosopher has ever openly revealed this Secret Fire, and this powerful agent, which works all the wonders of the Art : he who shall not understand it, and not know how to distinguish it by the characters whereby it is described, ought to make a stand here, and pray to God to make it clear to him : for the knowledge of this Great Secret is rather a gift of Heaven, than a Light acquired by the natural force of reasoning ; let him nevertheless read the writings of the philosophers; let him meditate ; and above all things let him pray : there is no difficulty which may not in the end be made clear by Work, Meditation and Prayer. Without the sublimation of the Stone, the conversion of the Elements and the extraction of the Principles is impossible ; and this conversion . . . is the only way whereby our Mercury can be prepared. Apply yourselves therefore to know this Secret Fire, which dissolves the Stone naturally and without violence, and makes it dissolve into Water in the great sea of the Wise."

This is, perhaps, more enlightening for those who have some Qabalistic training—and indeed it is our opinion that Alchemy is virtually a closed book for those who have not some such key to help them—and for the benefit of those who have not, we would point out that the Great Sea is a title of Binah, the Great Mother Supernal, the third Sephira, whose analogue in the divisions of the Soul is Neshamah. To this Sephira is also referred—in the Alchemical Qabalistic Treatise known as Ash Mezareph or the Purifying Fire—Sulphur, whose fiery nature causes it to be used frequently as the symbol of the Secret Fire of the Adepts. If then we take the compound of the Stone as Salt, we have here brought together the three well-known principles of Salt, Sulphur and Mercury.

And if it should be objected that we have but slight grounds for assuming salt to be thus referred, we reply that we have the support of Khunrath in his *Amphi-theatrum*. "The philosopher's stone," he says, " is

88

Ruach Elohim, which moved upon the face of the waters, the firmament being in the midst, conceived and made body, truly and sensibly, in the virgin womb of the greater world, namely that Earth which is without form and water. The Son, born into the light of the Macrocosm, mean and of no account in the eyes of the vulgar, consubstantial nevertheless, and like his father the lesser world, setting aside all idea of anything individually human : universal, triune, hermaphrodite ; visible, sensible to hearing, to smell, local and finite ; made manifest by itself regeneratively by the obstetric hand of the Physico-Chemical Art : glorified in his once assumed body, for benefits and uses almost infinite ; wonderfully salutary to the microcosm and to the macrocosm in universal triunity. The Salt of Saturn, the Universal son of Nature, has reigned, does reign, and will reign naturally and universally in all things ; always and everywhere universal through its own fusibility, self-existent in nature. Hear and attend ! SALT, that most ancient principle of the Stone ; whose nucleus in the Decad guard in holy silence. Let him who hath understanding understand ; I have spoken it—not without weighty cause has Salt been dignified with the name of Wisdom : than which, together with the SUN, nothing is found more useful."

Considering the foregoing and remembering what Basil Valentine has told us in previous chapters, the nature of this solution should now be getting tolerably clear, nevertheless the descriptions given are so helpful in the incidental information that we may gain from them, that we will venture to give two, the first of which will be from the same source as that we have just concluded.

" In the first act of the physico-chemical works," says Khunrath, " by diverse instruments and labours and the various artifice of the Hands and Fire, from Adrop (which in its proper tongue is called Saturn., i.e., the Lead of the Wise) "—and is thus the prime matter of the Stone, Salt, Saturn and Lead being alternatively interchangeable in their reference to Chokmah, the second Sephira—" our heart of Saturn, the bonds of coagulation being dextrously released, the Green Duenech and the Vitriol of Venus, which are the true matters of the Blessed Stone will appear. The Green Lion, lurking and concealed, is drawn forth from the Cavern of his Saturnine Hill by attractions and allurements suitable to his nature. All the blood copiously flowing from his wounds, by the acute lance transfixed, is diligently collected, ule and lili ; the mud earth, wet, humid, stagnant, impure, partaking of Adam, the First Matter of the creation of the Greater World of our very selves and of our potent Stone, is made manifest—the Wine which the Wise have called the Blood of the Earth, which likewise is the Red of Lully, so named on account of its tincture,

90

which is the colour of its virtue, thick, dense and black, blacker than black, will then be at hand ; the bond by which the soul is tied to the body and united together with it into one substance is relaxed and dissolved. The Spirit and the Soul by degrees depart from the body and are separated step by step ; whilst this takes place the fixed is made volatile, and the impure body (of the Spirit) from day to day is consumed, is destroyed, dies, blackens and goes to Ashes. These Ashes, my Son, deem not of little worth ; they are the diadem of thy body ; in them lies our pigmy, conquering and destroying giants."

If much of the symbolism of the above seems too involved for the taste of some, our second quotation should appeal to them more. On the statement of Thomas Vaughan it is from another Frater R.C., who was known by the title of Sapiens, and avoids much of the usual terminology of the Alchemists. " The state of true being," he says, " is that from which nothing is absent ; to which nothing is added and nothing still less can harm. All needful is that with which no one can dispense. Truth is therefore the highest excellence and an impregnable fortress, having few friends and beset by innumerable enemies, though invisible in these days to almost the whole world, but an invincible security to those who possess it. In this citadel is contained that true and indubitable Stone and Treasure of Philosophers, which uneaten by moths

and unpierced by thieves remaineth to eternity—
though all things else dissolve—set up for the ruin of
many and the salvation of some.

"This matter which for the crowd is vile, exceedingly contemptible and odious, yet not hateful but
loveable and precious to the wise, beyond gems and
tried gold. A lover itself of all, to all well-nigh an
enemy, to be found everywhere, yet discovered scarcely
by any, though it cries through the streets to all : Come
to me all ye who seek and I will lead you in the true
path. This is that only thing proclaimed by the true
philosophers, that which overcometh all and is itself
overcome by nothing, searching heart and body,
penetrating whatsoever is stony and stiff, consolidating
that which is weak, establishing resistance in the hard.

"It confronts us all, though we see it not, crying and
proclaiming with uplifted voice : I am the way of
truth ; see that ye walk therein, for there is no other
path unto life : yet we do not all hearken unto her.
She giveth forth an odour of sweetness, and yet we
perceive it not. Daily and freely at her feasts she
offers herself to us in sweetness, but we will not taste
and see. Softly she draws us towards salvation and
still we reject her yoke. For we are become as stones,
having eyes and not seeing, ears and not hearing,
nostrils refusing to smell, a tongue that will not speak,
a mouth that will not taste, feet which refuse to walk
and hands that work at nothing. O miserable race of

men, which are not superior to stones, yea, so much the more inferior because to the one and not to the other is given knowledge of their acts. Be ye transmuted— she cries—be ye transmuted from dead stones into living philosophical stones. I am the true Medicine, rectifying and transmuting that which is no longer into that which it was before corruption entered, and into something better by far, and that which is no longer into that which it ought to be. Lo, I am at the door of your conscience, knocking night and day, and ye will not open unto me. Yet I wait mildly ; I do not depart in anger ; I suffer your affronts patiently, hoping thereby to lead you where I seek to bring. Come again, and come again often, ye who seek wisdom: buy without money and without price, not with gold and silver, nor yet by your own labours that which is offered freely.

" O sonorous voice, O voice sweet and gracious to ears of sages. O fount of inexhaustible riches to those who are searching after truth and justice. O consolation to those who are desolate. What seek ye further, ye anxious mortals ? Why torment your minds with innumerable anxieties, ye miserable ones ? Prithee, what madness blinds you, when within and not without you is all that you seek outside instead of within you ? Such is the peculiar vice of the vulgar, that despising their own, they desire ever what is foreign, nor yet altogether unreasonably, for of ourselves we have nothing that is good. Or if indeed we possess any, it is received from Him Who alone is eternal good. On the contrary our disobedience hath appropriated that which is evil within us from an evil principle without, and beyond this evil thus possessed within him, man has nothing of his own; for whatsoever is good in his nature belongs to the Lord of goodness. At the same time that is counted to him as his own which he receives from the Good Principle. Albeit dimly that Life which is the Light of men shineth in the darkness within us, a Life which is not of us, but of Him Who hath it from everlasting. He hath planted it in us, that in His Light Who dwelleth in Light inaccessible, we may behold the Light. Herein we surpass the rest of His creatures; thus are we fashioned in His likeness, Who hath given us a beam of His own inherent Light. Truth must not therefore be sought in our natural self, but in this likeness of God within us.

" True knowledge begins when after a comparison of the imperishable with the perishable, of life and annihilation, the soul—yielding to the superior attraction of what is eternal—doth elect to be made one with the higher soul. The Mind emerges from that knowledge and as a beginning chooses voluntary separation of the body, beholding with the soul, on the one hand, the foulness and corruption of the body, and on the other the everlasting splendour and felicity of the higher soul. Being moved thereto by the Divine inbreathing, and neglecting things of flesh, it yearns to be connected with the soul, and that alone desires which it finds comprehended by God in salvation and glory. But the body itself is brought to harmonise with the union of both. This is that wonderful philosophical transmutation of body into spirit and spirit into body about which an instruction has come down to us from the wise of old : ' Fix that which is volatile and volatilise that which is fixed ; and thou shalt obtain our Mastery.' That is to say : Make the stiff-necked body tractable, and the virtue of the higher soul herself, shall communicate invariable constancy to the material part so that it will abide all tests. Gold is tried by fire, and by this process all that is not gold is cast out. O pre-eminent gold of the philosophers, with which the Sons of the Wise are enriched, not with that which is coined.

" Come hither, ye who seek after so many ways the Treasure of the Philosophers. Behold that Stone which ye have rejected, and learn first what it is before you go to seek it. It is more astonishing than any miracle that a man should desire after that which he does not know. It is a folly to go in quest of that, the truth of which the investigators do not know ; such a search is hopeless. I counsel therefore all and sundry scrutators that they should ascertain in the first place whether that which they look for exists before they start on their travels; they will not be frustrated then in their attempts. The wise man seeks what he loves and loves only that which he knows : otherwise he would be a fool. Out of knowledge therefore cometh love, the Truth of all, which alone is esteemed by all just philosophers.

"Ye toil in vain, all exposers of hidden secrets in Nature when—taking another path than is—ye endeavour to discover by material means the powers of material things. Learn therefore to know Heaven by Heaven, not by earth, but the powers of that which is material discern by that which is heavenly. No one can ascend to that Heaven which is sought by you unless He Who came down from a Heaven which you seek shall not first enlighten. Ye seek an incorruptible Medicine, which shall not only transmute the body from corruption into a perfect mode but so preserve it continually ; yet except in Heaven itself, never anywhere will you discover it. The celestial virtue, by invisible rays meeting at the centre of the earth, penetrates all elements and generates and maintains elementated things. No one can be brought to birth therein save in the likeness of that which is also drawn therefrom. The combined foetus of both parents is so preserved in Nature that both parents may be recognisable therein, in potentiality and in act.

"What shall cleave more closely than the Stone in philosophical generation ? Learn from within thyself

to know whatsoever is in Heaven and on earth, that
thou mayest become wise in all things. Thou seest
not that Heaven and the elements were once but one
substance and were separated one from the other by
Divine skill for the generation of thyself and all that
is. Didst thou know this, the rest could not escape,
unless indeed thou art devoid of all capacity. Again, in
every generation such a separation is necessary as I
have said must be made by thee before starting out
in the study of true philosophy. Thou wilt never
make out of others that one thing which thou needest
unless first thou shalt make out of thyself that one of
which thou hast heard. For such is the will of God,
that the pious should perform the work which they
desire, and the perfect fulfil another on which they are
bent. To men of bad will there shall be no harvest
other than they have sown; furthermore, on account
of their malice, their good seed shall be changed very
often into cockle. Perform, then, the work which
thou seekest in such a manner that so far as may be
in thy power, thou mayst escape a like misfortune.

"So do therefore, my soul and my body: rise up
now and follow your higher soul. Let us go up into
that high mountain before us, from the pinnacle of
which I will show you that place where two ways meet,
of which Pythagoras spoke in cloud and darkness.
Our eyes are opened; now shines the Sun of Holiness
and Justice, guided by which we cannot turn aside

from the way of truth. Let thine eyes look first upon the right path, lest they behold vanity before wisdom is perceived. See you not that shining and impregnable tower? Therein is Philosophical Love, a fountain from which flow living waters, and he who drinks thereof shall thirst no more after vanity. From that most pleasant and delectable place goes a plain path to one more delightful still, wherein Wisdom draws the yoke. Out of her fountain flow waters far more blessed than the first, for if our enemies drink thereof it is necessary to make peace with them. Most of those who attain here direct their course still further, but not all attain the end. It is such a place which mortals may scarcely reach unless they are raised by the Divine Will to the state of immortality; and then, or ever they enter, they must put off the world, the hindering vesture of fallen life.

" In those who attain hereto there is no longer any fear of death; on the contrary they welcome it daily with more willingness, judging that whatsoever is agreeable in the natural order is worthy of their acceptance. Whosoever advances beyond these three regions passes from the sight of men. If so be that it be granted us to see the second and the third, let us seek to go no further. Behold, beyond the first and crystalline arch, a second arch of silver, beyond which there is a third of adamant. But the fourth comes not within our vision till the third lies behind us. This is the golden realm of abiding happiness, void of care, filled with perpetual joy."

This solution, we may then judge, was a dissolution or loosening of the vital bond—but not a breaking of it —whereby the soul or spirit, or soul and spirit, might be freed from the body and its bondage, whence arose, presumably, that teaching of Plato and Plotinus that it is the business of philosophers to study how to be dead, explained by Porphyry, who says that " there is a twofold death, the one, indeed, universally known, in which the body is liberated from the soul ; but the other peculiar to the philosophers, in which the soul is liberated from the body."

This, of course, will involve us in a consideration of the mantic states of the mysteries, but we prefer to postpone this to our study of the second stage of the Subtle Work, devoting our attention in the meantime to the first stage, Conversion.

CHAPTER XI

"CONVERT the elements," says Arnold, "and you will find what you seek ; for our operation is nothing else than a mutation of natures, and the method of conversion in our Argent Vive is the reduction of natures to their first root."

Conversion is a curious word, and is usually taken to mean a changing from one state or thing to another. The ordinary meaning of the Latin *converto* from which it is derived is to turn round, and we take it that when the Alchemists spoke of this conversion as part of the process, they meant that for a true and perfect manifestation the natural order of procedure ought to be turned round or introverted. It also implies the sense con-version, meaning the imposing of a Higher Order on one's own nature, but this is rather the object than the method.

Now the natural procedure is the descent into matter and the ascent out of it, while the Hermetic process involves an inversion, or more properly a conversion or turning round of this, so that by converting you reduce it back into its first original, but plus the intensification brought about by evolution

100

and experience, bringing it back again afterwards into a fresh reunion with its caput mortuum.

This, of course, foreshadows the two remaining processes, of the Subtle Work, but as we have already pointed out, there is no exact and sharp division anywhere, as each stage, after the first, involves both those which have preceded it and those which are to follow.

It is not, therefore, necessary to linger over this process, but to pass on to the next stage, Separation, of which Paracelsus says that it is "the greatest miracle in philosophy, and that magic the most singular by which it is accomplished; very excellent for quickness of penetration and swiftness of operation, the like whereof Nature knows not."

In one of his indirect allusions to this part of the work, Vaughan, in the introduction to his *Anthroposophia*, tells us that the soul "Hath many ways to break up her house, but her best is without a disease. This is her mystical walk, an exit only to return. When she takes the air at this door, it is without prejudice to her tenement."

Sendivogius, in his *New Light of Alchemy*, says that "The searcher of this Sacred Science knows that the soul in man, the lesser world or microcosm, substituting the place of its centre, is the king, and is placed in the vital spirit in the purest blood. That governs the mind, and the mind the body; but this same soul . . .

which operates in the body, governing all its motions, hath a far greater operation out of the body, because out of the body it absolutely reigns."

And Vaughan, in the latter part of the *Anthroposophia Theomagica,* confirms this, telling us that whereas while enclosed in the body she imagines whatever she will, " If she were once out of the body she could act all that she imagined. ' In a moment,' saith Agrippa, ' whatsoever she desires, that shall follow.' In this state she can ' act upon the macrocosm,' make general commotion in the two spheres of air and water, and alter the complexions of times. Neither is this a fable, but the unanimous finding of the Arabians, with the two princes Avicebron and Avicenna. She hath then an absolute power in miraculous and more than natural transmutations. She can in an instant transfer her own vessel from one place to another. She can— by an union with universal force—infuse and communicate her thoughts to the absent, be the distance never so great. Neither is there anything under the sun but she may know it, and—remaining only in one place— she can acquaint herself with the actions of all places whatsoever. I omit to speak of her magnet, wherewith she can attract all things—as well spiritual as natural. ' Finally ' " (says Agrippa) " ' there is no work in the whole course of Nature, however arduous, however excellent, however supernatural it may be, that the human soul, when it has attained the source of its divinity—which the Magi term the soul standing and not falling—cannot accomplish by its own power and apart from any external help.' But who is he—amidst so many thousand philosophers—that knows her nature substantially and the genuine, specifical use thereof? This is Abraham's ' great secret, wonderful exceedingly, and deeply hidden, sealed with six seals, and out of these proceed fire, water and air, which are divided into males and females.' " (Sepher Yetzirah, Cap. iii, sect. 2.) " We should therefore pray continually that God would open our eyes, whereby we might see to employ that talent which He hath bestowed upon us but lies buried now in the ground and doth not fructify at all. He it is to whom we must be united by ' an essential compact' and then we shall know all things ' show forth openly by clear vision in the Divine Light.' "

Vaughan, apart from his great admiration of those whom he terms " The most Illustrious and Truly Regenerated Brethren R.C.," was a great adherent of Agrippa, and we may therefore venture to give an extract from this source, which we do not find in Vaughan's works. It is taken from the *Third Book of Occult Philosophy*, and bears immediately upon our context.

He tells us that the soul of man, being estranged from the corporeal senses, adheres to a divine nature from which it receives those things which it cannot search into by its own proper power : for when the mind is free, the reins of the body being loosed, and going forth as out of a close prison, it transcends the bonds of the members, and, nothing hindering, being stirred up in its proper essence comprehends all things. And therefore was man said to be made in the express image of God, seeing that he contains the Universal Reason within himself, and has a corporeal similitude also with all. Whosoever, therefore, shall know himself, shall know all things in himself, but especially he shall know God, according to whose image he was made.

This, then, we may conclude, is the Death alluded to by Pythagoras in the Eighth Dictum of the *Turba*, where he says that it " consists in the separation of the soul from the body."

We are thus led to a plain understanding of one of the profound mysteries of Alchemy, perhaps the greatest and most profound, continually revealed by them, and as continually obscured again, but quite unmistakable if we do not wilfully refuse to see. And as it deals with the mantic states of mystic trance, it was usually accompanied by stringent warnings as to its dangers.

These are twofold, for not the least among them are those which await the unenlightened experimenter, who, not understanding the nature of the trance state that he endeavours to induce, adopts methods that are undesirable in the extreme. Following these are the dangers that await even the aspirant who may have discovered the right road, but penetrates, as it were, into a strange country of whose ways and inhabitants he is completely and woefully ignorant.

So great are both these categories, that we do not feel justified in pursuing our inquiry further without devoting some small space to a consideration of them.

Among the first class of risk that we have enumerated is that of being misled into the supposition that mesmerism or hypnotism has anything to do with the sacred trance. At first sight this is quite a plausible hypothesis, and some modern writers have devoted considerable space to elaborating the remarks of the Alchemists concerning the "Work of the hands" into arguments in favour of such a supposition.

We cannot too strongly repudiate and condemn any such suggestion, which, to our way of thinking, is pestilent in the extreme, sapping, as it does, the very faculty which it is most desirable should be fostered in the subject, the Will, which is the precious Salt, Lead or Saturn of the Adepts. Apart from which the states of lucidity achieved by such methods differ fundamentally from those at which we are aiming.

Neither can we admit as much more desirable the practice of inducing auto-hypnotic states by the prolonged staring at talismans and symbols, or in placing these upon the forehead in an attempt to obtain visions. Allied with these methods, we would also strongly discourage the student from such other methods as gazing into crystals, bowls of water or ink, magical mirrors and the like, which may, indeed, produce in certain subjects a degree of mediumship, but nothing more, and mediumship is not what we are seeking.

Lastly, and most emphatically, we would warn any-one against attempting any of the invocations or evocations of talismanic and ceremonial magic as set forth in the textbooks and grimoires dealing with this subject. The results, if any are achieved—and unfortunately they can be—are likely to be exceedingly unpleasant and dangerous.

Even where the results obtained by the methods outlined in the three preceding paragraphs are not actually dangerous, they are not likely to be useful, but, on the contrary, are almost certain to be misleading. In illustration of which statement we will quote a few extracts from Iamblichos, who, in his work on the Egyptian Mysteries, deals exclusively with Theurgic Magic.

He tells us that " When there occurs some errancy in the theurgic technique "—as when, for example, some published textbook on Magic is used, which, if it be not purely evil, is admittedly defective somewhere —" the Images which ought to be at the Autopsia are not, but others of a different kind. These, the inferiors, assume the guise of the more venerable orders, and pretend to be the very ones which they are counterfeiting, and there will be a great mass of falsehood flow forth from the perversion.

"We say the same things now in regard to phantasms or apparitions. For if these are not themselves genuine, but others of the kind are so, that really exist, they certainly will not be among the self-revealing spirits, but are of the kind that display themselves ostentatiously as genuine. These participate in deception and falsehood after the manner of the forms that appear in mirrors, and attract the understanding to no good purpose in regard to matters . . . that will be among fraudulent deceptions. . . . On the other hand the gods and those that come after the gods reveal true likenesses of themselves, but never project apparitions such as are formed in water or in mirrors.

"Thou mayst not associate in the mind the spectacles of the gods that are superlatively efficacious with the apparitions got up by technical magic. For the latter have neither the energy nor the essence nor the genuineness of the objects that are beheld, but only project bare phantasms that seem real.

"I shall wonder if any one of the theurgic priests who behold the genuine, ideal forms of the gods should consent to allow them at all. For why should anyone consent to take idola or spectral figures in exchange for those that have real being, and be carried from the very first to the last and lowest? Do we not know that all things which are brought into view by such a mode . . . are really phantoms of what is genuine, and that they appear good to the seeing, but never are really so?

" The individual creating the spectral figures employs in his procedures neither the revolutions of the heavenly bodies nor the powers that exist in them by nature; and in short he is not able to come in contact with them. But as he follows an art, and does not proceed theurgically, he deals with the last and most inferior emanations, manifestly, from their nature, about the extreme part of the universe.

" The projector of spectral figures trusts in spectres destitute of soul, only animated with the outward appearance of life, holding together externally a framework of diversified complexion, and absolutely ephemeral in duration. Nothing of the things thus fashioned by man is unalloyed and pure. They are wanting in all, being brought together from manifold and incompatible substances. When any such multitude of auras accumulated from many sources has been mingled together, it is shown to be feeble and fleeting. They vanish more quickly than the idola seen in mirrors. For when the incense is placed upon the altar, the figure is immediately formed from the vapour as it is carried upwards, but when the vapour becomes mingled and dispersed into the whole atmosphere, the idolon is immediately dissolved and not a trace of it remains.

THEURGY

" Why then should this juggling be desired by the
man that loves manifestations that are true? If they
know that these things about which they are engaged
are structures formed of passive material, the evil
would be a simple matter. . . . But if they hold to
these spectral figures as to gods, the absurdity will not
be utterable in speech or endurable in act. For into
such a soul the divine ray never shines ; for it is not in
the nature of things for it to be bestowed upon objects
that are wholly repugnant, and those that are held fast
by dark phantasms have no place for its reception.
Such-like wonder-making with phantasms will, therefore, be in the same category with shadows that are
very far from the truth."

The second class of dangers should be tolerably
obvious from what we have already indicated, but not
the least of them is illusion. As, however, we shall
have to deal with these in our consideration of the
nature of the trance state, we will not now dwell
further upon them.

CHAPTER XII

WE now, therefore, come to the trance state itself, and it should by now be abundantly clear that by this we mean the sacred state of divine trance, and not any psychic, somnambulistic or hypnotic states.

The principal characteristic of the mantic trance, as it is frequently called, is that in every stage of it complete self-consciousness and self-control are retained, although there is obtained what Plato calls a "divine release from the ordinary ways of men."

The earlier stages are sometimes called muesis, from muo, to close the eyes, for, as Synesius says in the *Aegyptiacus*, "There are two sets of eyes in the Mysteries. The Lower are closed when the Higher are opened," a statement that has misled many into speculations regarding hypnotism that we have before mentioned.

These states are connected with the noetic nature and lead naturally to the knowledge of spiritual realities and the acquirement of certain powers ; and they are designed to lead up to and culminate in the true re-birth, the birth from above as it is often called.

THEURGY

Though self-consciousness is maintained, the mind is drawn away from the things of sense, the spiritual sight, hearing and so forth becoming stimulated when, as the Oracle describes it, " No longer are visible unto thee the Vault of the Heavens, the Mass of the Earth ; when for thee the Stars have lost their Light and the Lamp of the Moon is veiled and around thee is the Lightning Flash."

Yet until, as we have repeatedly emphasised, the mind and body have been as far as possible purified by prayer and meditation and the pursuance of the Sacred Rites, the danger remains that the phrenic, lower or psychic nature may play an undesired part and lead to illusions and self-deceptions, which are described as intrusive figures from the Underworld, seeking to draw away the attention of the candidate from the truth.

Ancient and mediæval writings are full of descriptions of these appearances, which are even said to have material efficacy in Divine works under the guidance of those who understand and can control them ; whence the saying of the Oracle, " Nature persuadeth us that there are pure Demons, and that the germinations even of evil matter can be alike useful and good."

Nevertheless the soul is liable to be led away into oblivion by these in the early stages, so that the further injunction is necessary, " Let the immortal depth of thy soul be predominant, and all thine eyes extend upwards. Stoop not down, for a precipice lieth beneath the Earth, drawing through the ladder which hath seven steps, beneath which is the Throne of dire Necessity."

This is why Vaughan, speaking of the First Matter, says, " The eye of man never saw her twice under one and the same shape." And Lully, that the first principles of the Art are " Fugitive Spirits, condensed in air, in shape like divers monsters, beasts and men, which move like clouds hither and thither."

But apart from such apparitions, there are more subtle forms of illusion arising from memory, desire, imagination, emotion and so forth, which, while not necessarily alarming, and probably not tending to arouse the suspicions in any way, are at the same time totally inaccurate and misleading.

The following letter quoted by Vaughan in his *Lumen de Lumine* as being from the Fratres R.C., bears on all these points in a most interesting manner. We give only the middle portion of the letter, which is the part that actually illustrates them. It runs as follows :

" There is a mountain situated in the midst of the earth or centre of the world, which is both small and great. It is soft, also above measure hard and strong. It is far off and near at hand, but by the providence of God it is invisible. In it are hidden most ample treasures, which the world is not able to value. This mountain, by envy of the devil, who always opposes the

Glory of God and the felicity of man, is compassed about with very cruel beasts and ravenous birds, which make the way thereto both difficult and dangerous; and therefore hitherto, because the time is not yet come, the way thither could not be sought after nor found out. But now at last the way is to be found by those that are worthy—but notwithstanding by every man's self-labour and endeavour.

"To this mountain shall you go in a certain night when it comes most long and dark; and see that you prepare yourselves by prayer. Insist upon the way that leads to the mountain, but ask not of any man where it lies, only follow your guide, who will offer himself to you and will meet you in the way. Truly you shall not fail to know him.

"This guide shall bring you to the mountain at midnight, when all things are silent and dark. It is necessary that you arm yourself with a resolute, heroic courage, lest you fear those things that will happen and fall back. You need no sword or other bodily weapons, only call upon your God sincerely and from the depths of your mind.

"When you have discovered the mountain, the first miracle that will happen is this: A most vehement and very great wind that will shake the whole mountain and shatter the rocks to pieces. You will be encountered then by dragons, lions and other terrible wild beasts; but fear not any of these things. Be resolute

H   113 and take heed that you return not, for your guide, who brought you hither, will not suffer any evil to befall you. As for the treasure, it is not yet discovered, but it is very near.

" After this wind will come an earthquake, which will overthrow those things that the wind had left, and make all flat. Be sure you fall not off.

" The earthquake being passed there will follow a fire that will consume all the earthly rubbish and discover the treasure. But as yet you cannot see it. After all these things and near daybreak, there shall be a great calm, and you shall see the Day-Star arise and the dawning will appear and you shall perceive a great treasure.

" The chiefest thing in it and the most perfect, is a certain exalted tincture, with which, if it served God and were worthy of such gifts, the whole world might be tinged and turned into most pure gold."

Now these states of Manteia were in no sense haphazard or undirected; for before venturing far, if at all, with them, the aspirant was supposed, as we have already indicated, to study carefully the theoretical aspects of what he was to do, and to familiarise himself with the systems of cosmogony and cosmology held by the school in which he was studying, as far as any such system could be grasped theoretically. Also it was necessary for him to have some academic acquaintance with the Orders and Hierarchies of

THEURGY

Essences he was about to encounter, together with the tokens and signs by which he might recognise and be recognised, and by virtue of which he might claim such instruction and enlightenment as his degree of spiritual attainment would enable him to assimilate.

And it should be clearly understood that the Hierophants and candidates of the true Mystery Schools were no mere dilettante dabblers and experimenters, satisfied with visions of the Astral World, or the planes immediately contiguous to ours, against which they were warned by the Oracle in no uncertain terms :

" Stoop not down into the Darkly Splendid World, wherein continually lieth a faithless depth, and Hades wrapped in clouds, delighting in unintelligible images ; precipitous, winding ; a black ever-rolling abyss, ever espousing a Body unluminous, formless and void."

They sought to penetrate into the further Worlds, the Yetziratic and even Briatic, and to rise ever higher through them until they beheld the Divine Light, that Light which was formless, which was the true stage of Epopteia or Beholding.

Although we are not considering the Eastern views on these subjects in this short survey, nevertheless the following descriptions of this Light, taken from the *Bardo Thödol*, or Thibetan *Book of the Dead*, are so apt that we do not hesitate to give them.

" Thy guru hath set thee face to face before with the

Clear Light ; and now thou art about to experience it in its Reality in the Bardo state, wherein all things are like the void and cloudless sky, and the naked, spotless intellect is like unto a transparent vacuum without circumference or centre. At this moment know thyself and abide in that state. . . . Now thou art experiencing the Radiance of the Clear Light of Pure Reality. Recognise it. . . . Thy present intellect, in real nature void, not formed into anything as regards characteristics or colour, naturally void, is the very Reality, the All-Good. . . . Thine own consciousness, shining void and inseparable from the Great Body of Radiance, hath no birth nor death and is the Immutable Light."

But to reach any of these states, or even to assist in the preliminary purifications, the practice of the exercises of the Mysteries was necessary, which were in some measure connected with the process of solution or separation that we have been discussing. And in this connection we ought perhaps to mention an error that appears to be very prevalent concerning them. We have already dealt with it to some extent in Chapters III and IV, though limiting it at the time to sex practices.

We would now, therefore, extend this to physical exercises generally, such as one reads of in certain forms of yoga. The exercises of the Mysteries of Greece and Egypt were of a different order, being

116

purely spiritual, and were intimately connected with that ritual which was a preliminary to the earlier mantic states. They were neither physical nor intellectual, but were linked with the Alchemical volatilising of the fixed and fixing of the volatile with which we have all along been dealing, and with which we shall deal again, both in the next stage of the Subtle Work, and in the section on dew which summarises the whole procedure.

When Synesius says " Intellect above all things separates whatever is contrary to the true purity of the phantastic Spirit ; for it attenuates this spirit in an occult and ineffable manner, and extends it to Divinity," he is not speaking of the natural intellect, which cannot do this, but of the Mind in the sense which we have previously outlined in Chapter II. And with this clue we must, for the time being, remain content.

CHAPTER XIII

WE now come to the last of our three stages of
the Subtle Work, which we have termed
Reunion. This process is also the Alchemical Coagulation and the fixing of the volatile. As the Smaragdine
Tablet says, " The power of it is integral if it be turned
into earth." And Senior, that " the highest fume
should be reduced to the lowest; for the divine
water is the thing descending from heaven, the
reducer of the soul to its body, which it at length
revives."

And Trismosin, after discussing the putrefaction
and decoction, quotes Hermes as saying, " It is
indeed needful that at the end of this World, Heaven
and Earth should meet and come home." And again,
in the Fourth Parable of his *Splendor Solis*, he quotes
Senior thus : " The Spirit dissolves the body and in the
Dissolution extracts the Soul of the Body, and changes
this body into Soul, and the Soul is changed into
Spirit, and the Spirit is again added to the Body, for
thus it has stability."

Khunrath, likewise, in his *Amphitheatrum* informs
us concerning the whole of the second or Subtle Work

as follows : "In the Second Operation, which takes place in one circular, crystalline vessel, justly proportioned to the quality of its contents, also in one theosophic, cabalistically sealed furnace or Athanor, and by one fire, the body, soul and spirit, externally washed and cleansed and purged with the most accurate diligence and Herculean labours, and again compounded, commingle, rot of themselves and without manual co-operation, by the sole labours of nature, are dissolved, conjoined and reunited ; and thus the fixed becomes volatile wholly ; these three principles also are of themselves coagulated, diversifiedly coloured, calcined and fixed ; and hence the world arises renovated and new."

While Eudoxus, in his Fourth Key—if we may be pardoned for thus multiplying authorities—says : "The Fourth Key of the Art is the entrance to the Second Work (and a reiteration in part and development of the foregoing) : it is this which reduces our Water into Earth ; there is but this only Water in the World, which by a bare boiling can be converted into Earth, because the Mercury of the Wise carries in its centre its own Sulphur which coagulates it. The terrification of the Spirit is the only operation of this work. Boil them with patience ; if you have proceeded well, you will not be a long time without perceiving the marks of this coagulation ; and if they appear not in their time they will never appear ; because it is an undoubted sign that you have failed in some essential thing in the former operations ; for to corporify the Spirit, which is our Mercury, you must have well dissolved the body in which the Sulphur which coagulates the Mercury is enclosed. But Hermes assumes that our mercurial water shall obtain all the virtues which the philosophers attribute to it if it be turned into earth. An earth admirable is it for fertility—the Land of Promise of the Wise, who, knowing how to make the dew of Heaven fall upon it, cause it to produce fruits of inestimable price. Cultivate then diligently this precious earth, moisten it often with its own humidity, dry it as often, and you will no less augment its virtue than its weight and its fertility."

And this in part is the meaning of the fable of Osiris, who, his parts having been gathered together again and preserved in a chest floating upon the waters of the Nile for a time, emerged therefrom resuscitated, and came forth immune from all ills or harm and beyond all comparison more powerful than before.

In short this reunion is the key to the Mystical Rebirth in the deathless Solar Body, admirably preluded in a quotation from the lost Gospel of Phillip given by Epiphanius, " I have united myself, assembling myself together from the four quarters of the universe, and joining together the members that were scattered abroad," and elaborated in the Apocalypse in the allegory of the birth of the Man-child.

For the whole process we have been studying is manifestly connected with the attainment by the soul of the candidate to the highest level to which his spiritual development can aspire, and by the absorption of the soul when in this state of all the wisdom, power and purifying energy which it can assimilate. It then returns to the body, which is its proper earth, purging it by the radiations of the energy thus acquired.

This process being constantly repeated, the level is gradually raised, for the purging at each return ensures further projection at the next solution, which is the augmentation of the power of the stone which is so much spoken of in the later stages of the work.

Thus the purifying and vivifying energy is absorbed in ever increasing amounts, while at the same time the power of maintaining the contacts is steadily developed, which also assists in the general growth of the soul.

In such a manner, by successive stages, the aspirant is said to progress towards union with his Higher Self, and because of these various stages of development, there were different forms of the sacred rites. This not unnaturally adds to the difficulties of gleaning any information relative to them, for the records do not in any way plainly set them forth by stages, but intermingle the accounts the one with the other, as the Alchemists at all events admit quite openly, so that their meaning shall remain unintelligible to those without the Key.

We have above mentioned the augmentation of the stone, which we have seen to be intimately connected with the constant repetitions of the process. Eudoxus is quite definite in this assertion, saying in his Sixth Key that "The Multiplication of the Stone is by reiteration of the same operation, which consists but in opening and shutting, dissolving and coagulating, imbibing and drying; whereby the virtues of the Stone are infinitely augmentable."

The others are unanimous in their agreement with this thesis, and indeed it should be so obvious to the ordinary intelligence that we will waste no more time on it.

It will perhaps be of assistance to the student in the course of his own researches if we devote some small space to the consideration of some of the commoner terms in use among the Alchemists, and in so doing we shall in a measure recapitulate and review what has gone before.

And if it should seem to anyone that according to our description of it, the work is shorter than they expected, it must not be forgotten that the fermentative process of the first work—and indeed all the processes of both works—has to be gone over again and again, repeatedly and with the greatest care. Hence the

Alchemists' command to the student to dissolve, distil, incerate, calcine, sublime, and fix the Occult Nature, and hence are we told that the Gold is to be tried seven times in the fire, so that the initial process alone comprises a death, a resurrection, a purification, a separation, an exaltation and a sublimation.

And in passing through the various stages, the First Matter, the Mercury of the Adepts, the Quintessence, is alluded to under a multitude of terms and by a variety of descriptions. As Agmon says in the concluding section of the *Turba*, which Arnold de Villa Nova borrowed for his *Speculum*, "It is also a stone and not a stone, spirit, soul and body ; it is white, volatile, concave, hairless, cold, and yet no one can apply the tongue with impunity to its surface. If you wish that it should fly, it flies ; if you say that it is water, you speak the truth ; if you say that it is not water, you speak falsely. Do not then be deceived by the multiplicity of names, but rest assured that it is one thing, unto which nothing alien is added. Investigate the place thereof, and add nothing foreign. Unless the names were multiplied, so that the vulgar might be deceived, many would deride our wisdom."

At times it is called an essential oil ; at others a sharp vinegar ; again a Dragon, a Chameleon, a Phœnix, a Salamander. Sometimes it is mineral, sometimes vegetable, sometimes animal ; now it is Fire or Light, then Earth, Air or Water ; at other times it is Magnesia,

Azoth, Antimony, Ether or Ens. Frequently it is resolved into its elements, or three component parts, Salt, Sulphur and Mercury, which are Spirit, Soul and Body ; Active, Passive and Resultant ; Father, Mother and Son ; Attraction, Repulsion and Circulation.

Planetary terms are frequently used. The Sun for the Active, the Moon for the Passive ; Saturn for the Self-willed Life, the Will at one stage of the operation ; Venus, the Celestial Light of Nature ; Vulcan, motion.

Again Salt is Will at another stage, whose analogue is Weight. The Brazen Body is the impure, natural born Spirit. The Orient Animal is the Will clothed in Light, which the Oracle describes as " Having put on the complete armed vigour of resounding Light, with triple strength fortifying the Soul and Mind."

The principle of Body is severally referred to as Caput Mortuum, Pigmy, Diadem of Body and Duenech.

The Vulture, Crow and Raven are synonymous terms for the Spirit of Life, though they appear to be used as indicative of different stages in the process, just as are the various colours so often alluded to.

The Philosophic Earth is that where the Magnesia, Terra Adamica or Red Root is sown ; where it dies and corrupts in order that it may renew itself as Salt. And here there appears to be a manifest contradiction, for the Earth of the Wise is another name for Mercury ; but this is nevertheless explicable, seeing that it conceives into itself the very seed, sperm or ferment by which it is nourished and brought to perfection.

The Red and White are Soul and Spirit, which emerge in union from the blackness of the mystical death, and we are told that when the Artist sees it he knows that he has the Great Arcanum.

Many interesting points arise from the consideration of Water, Air and Fire, and with these we will deal in the next chapter.

CHAPTER XIV

"IN the beginning the Elohim created the substance of the Heavens and the substance of the Earth. And the Earth was without form and void, and darkness was upon the face of the Abyss and the Ruach Elohim vibrated upon the face of the Waters."

Such are the first two verses of the Book Berashith—which we call Genesis—according to the Hebrew. On these words alone, and their implications and meanings, a book might be written, but we would only here draw the reader's attention to the word Ruach, whose implications we have to some extent discussed in an earlier chapter, adding here the fact that the gender of the word is feminine, which will explain some of the allusions in many of the previous quotations. Also to the words Abyss and Waters, which are both rendered by the same word in the Hebrew. This word is Thehom, and contains in itself the two ideas of " the formless " and " water," whence it might aptly be translated here as " formless waters."

This is the Virgin Water of the Alchemists, and Thomas Vaughan tells us that when the philosophers practised upon the Chaos itself, that is to say upon the

126

Formless and Void, they opened it and saw the Pre-existent Countenance of the Triad, and saw that all things here below, the Water of Mundane Life as it is elsewhere called, was a Thick Water, which is a term much used in Alchemy.

The apparent stark absurdity of the statement that the philosophers practised upon the Chaos will be elucidated later. For the moment we will consider this Thick Water. We find it mentioned in 2 Maccabees, i, 19-22, where the Sacred Fire was buried in a secret pit. On the return from the captivity it was found to have turned to a thick water, from which, however, the Fire was extracted.

In support of this analogy we find that the Sepher Yetzirah, or Book of Formation—which, as we have said, is one of the oldest books of the Qabalah, and is attributed by legend to Abraham, though its author in all probability was Rabbi Akiba—in describing the Creation says that Fire was derived from Water.

There is, of course, an obvious analogy between Thick Water and Gum, which is another term for it. It is also called White Mercury—Mercury giving quite a good parallel—and we note that there is a White Gum and that Permanent Water is White. Permanent Water is also called Igneous, while Mercury is Water of Sulphur, which may very well be taken to mean " containing Sulphur or Fire," and Hermes in the *Golden Treatise* says " Conserve in that Sea the Fire."

This Water, then, that is to say Permanent Water, is the First Matter, " which is that waterish substance which wets not the hands." " It looks like a Green Lizard," says Lully, " but its most prevalent colour is a certain inexpressible azure." Hereby he denotes its watery nature, both by the colour blue, and the fact that the Lizard probably represents Scorpio, which in good symbolism is Aquila, the Eagle, the Kerubic Emblem of Water and the Alchemical Emblem of Distillation. Lully continues, " The predominant element in it, however, is a certain fiery, subtle earth, whence it is often called earth, causing much confusion ; but this is the viscous or slimy part." And as it is said to be impregnated by the Sun it is spermatic and is called a Sperm of Earth.

This is also Sperm of the World, Catholic Magnesia, the Twofold Mercury or Azoth, Vinegar, Clean Water, Divine Water, Sea Water, Virgin's Milk and Mist. And here we would remind the student of the Mist that went up from the earth and watered the whole face of the ground mentioned in Gen. ii, 6.

We will now take the analogy of Gum, which gives us a good parallel—being a vegetable excretion—especially if we consider the idea of the Sperm or Seed just mentioned. This will also afford us the promised elucidation of the apparent absurdity of operating on the Chaos, for according to Vaughan the original Seminal Viscosity, Sperm or Seed from which the

128

World was made, disappeared in the Creation, for it was the Waters of Creation upon which the Spirit or Ruach Elohim brooded or vibrated in the beginning, transforming it into the World. The World, however, now yields us a secondary seed, which is the very same essence or substance with the primitive general one—the description of which, by the way, tallies rather well with ectoplasm. This Seed, says Vaughan, is abstracted in its heavenly, universal form by vegetables, which attract it at their roots as it comes from the air in Dew. This Sperm is generated from the mixture and marriage of the inferior and superior natures in the vapours.

Let no one be misled by any such statements into thinking that any common vegetables are meant, for it is quite otherwise. As well might the Tree of Life be mistaken in the same way. We are dealing here, as we have dealt all along, with one only thing; one matter, one vessel, one furnace, one laboratory.

But to resume. We have thus been led up to a consideration of Dew, a most important symbol, than which, perhaps, no better symbol of the Alchemical process can be quoted. The Alchemists, in their use of it, regard the air as a vast circulatory, whose upper reaches are extremely rarified. In it is involved all the idea of the action of opposites on one another, for fire and water, that is to say heat and moisture, are always busy with one another, and according to Anaxagoras in the *Turba*, the thickness or spermatic part of the fire falls into the air. The thickness or sperm of the air, and in it the thickness and sperm of the fire, falls into the water, and all these fall upon the earth, with which idea we should compare either body, soul and spirit, or the Qabalistic notion of the triple division of the soul as outlined in Chapter II.

Now the water is here to be taken as the middle nature between the air and the earth, the former, in ancient symbolism being hot and moist, and the latter cold and dry, while the water is cold and moist.

On a higher level the air is the reconciler between the water and the fire, so that thus the air becomes what we have already termed it, a vast circulatory where the inferiors and superiors meet like agent and patient, or, as some of the Alchemists express it, where Sulphur and Mercury are mingled.

Here things are said to be resolved into general principles by the action of wind, which is, of course, vibration, contrition and so forth. This resolves them into moisture, the prime element of creation, as it were, which then descends as dew, so that we have a perpetual rarefaction and condensation, or circular process going on, that which is generated in the air being taken up by the water, which acts as the body.

Now by dew, however, is not meant common dew, as with all substances treated of in Alchemy; but it serves to illustrate the sublimation of the volatile part, which, ascending, is acted upon by that which is its higher counterpart, of which it absorbs something, and then, becoming refixed, descends again into earth or body which it is able to some extent to purify, having been itself in some measure purified.

We have not treated this section in nearly as full a manner as it deserves, but it may nevertheless be seen from what we have said that water is sometimes called fire, and why this should be.

This fire involved in air, which is collected up by the water, is called Starry Milk or Air of Luna, so that water is like a flying bird, and the milky moisture which is found in her crystal breasts is called Milk of Birds, and thus some of the philosophers have said that " Birds do bring their Stone unto them." Fish are said to do the same thing, for they live in the Water.

And the air, which involves in itself a fire, is the Pneuma, Breath, Spirit or Ruach. But the symbol of Ruach Elohim is Fire, which, in the Soul is the Qabalistical Neshamah, the Higher part, by the Fire or Sulphur of which the Nephesch or lower part must be purged.

Now following the analogy of Dew and the evaporation of water from the earth into air, which it, as it were, dissolves and which contains fire, we must distil from the gross earth of our material natures the Nephesch, the subtle or watery part, which shall dissolve the volatile or airy part or Ruach, containing

131

the Fire, Neshamah. When this falls upon the earth as dew it will commence its purification.

There is in the Qabalah much about this Dew, but it is too technical for anything but a passing reference. It is said that from it the dead are raised up, and by dead is meant, in the mystical language of the Zohar, fallen.

To explain the sublimation of the essences with the matter in the foregoing, Vaughan and others postulate the Archeus or Central Sun, " For where the rays of the one and the other meet, the central, breaking through to meet the celestial, suffers a sort of ecstasy," says Vaughan, " So then, in winter, the face of the earth being as it were sealed, Magnesia is generated, but in spring and summer it ascends more freely."

This compounding of watery and airy natures has doubtless given rise to the term Green Stone, though some say it should be Green Lion. This curious beast is also the Poisonous Dragon of whom Hermes says in his *Golden Treatise*, " In every nature there is first the needful water, then the oily tincture and lastly the fœces or earth which remains below. But a Dragon inhabits all these, and they are his habitation, and the blackness is in them, and by it he ascends into the air. But while the fume remains in them they are not immortal. Take away, therefore, the vapour from the water, and the blackness from the oily tincture and death from the fœces ; and by distillation thou shalt

132

achieve a triumphant reward, even that in and by which the possessors live."

Now the Water, the Oil and the Earth are the hidden intrinsical natures, and in this sense every element is threefold. The Dragon is the self-willed spirit, as we have already said, which in its normal mode, resulting from the fall, is a poisonous nature and destroys all that it touches. This poison is the fume which is to be taken away. It is not one with the blackness which is in them, for this has a practical meaning linked with the dissolution at the end of the quotation, here given as distillation.

The oily tincture is Sulphur, for Hermes adds in the next paragraph, " The temperate unguent, which is Fire, is the medium between the fœces and the water, and is called the perscrutinator of the waters. For the unguents are called Sulphurs, because between fire and oil and the sulphurs there is close propinquity ; even as fire burns so does sulphur also."

The Dragon, to revert to him again, is salt in the impure state, also our Green Lion, so that this latter is synonymous with all those other terms which have been given in Chapter IV, and also with the Magical Earth, the Flos Salis Albi or Flower of White Salt, the White Sand and so on, for it is not specified always at what stage it is alluded to, and it must be borne in mind that in the Great Work nothing is added, only superfluities removed.

133

THEURGY

And this Magical Earth is that in which is the recreative fire, the " Land of Havilah where good gold is," which is Martian and Fiery. This is the Fire that coagulates the parts, and the Salt is the water that wets not the hands, the Magnesia that was exhibited in the Mysteries.

Thus we come at length to the end of our investigation, and we can but hope that it has not proved too disappointing to the reader, and that it will not be thought that too liberal a use has been made of quotations. Our object has been throughout to lead him to a study of this most fascinating and—as we consider it—all important subject, and to persuade him that the writings of the philosophers, despite their envious complexity, will well repay him for the pains to which he may be put in their perusal.

We may therefore, perhaps, be forgiven if we conclude by giving him two further extracts, which we will leave to his consideration without comment. The first is from the Fourth Parable of the *Splendor Solis* of Trismosin.

" This (Dissolution) the Philosophers give to understand in the following Signature or Figure : They saw a man black like a negro sticking fast in a black, dirty and foul smelling slime or clay ; to his assistance came a young woman, beautiful in countenance, and still more so in body, most handsomely adorned with many-coloured dresses, and she had wings on her back, the feathers of which were equal to those of the very finest white Peacock, and the quills were adorned with fine pearls, while the feathers reflected like golden mirrors. On her head she had a crown of pure gold, and on the top of it a silver star; around her neck she wore a necklace of fine gold, with the most precious Ruby, for which no king would be able to pay; her feet were clad with golden shoes, and from her was emanating the most splendid perfume, surpassing all aromas. She clothed the man with a purple robe and lifted him up to his brightest clearness, and took him with herself to Heaven."

The second is a recipe for the Medicine from Thomas Vaughan. This has unfortunately been described by a modern commentator in the following terms: "I must confess to a feeling that this recipe is a jest or a kind of parody on the ridiculous processes given by pretenders in Alchemy." We feel that the intelligent and not merely superficial reader will take a different view, and that the measure of his approval will indicate the measure of his understanding. It is given thus:

"℞. Ten parts of celestial slime. Separate the male from the female and then each from its earth, naturally, however, and without violence. Conjoin after separation in due, harmonic, vital proportion. The soul, descending straightway from the pyroplastic sphere, shall restore its dead and deserted body by a wonderful embrace. The conjoined substances shall be warmed by

135

a natural fire in a perfect marriage of spirit and body. Proceed according to the Vulcano-Magical Artifice till they are exalted into the Fifth Metaphysical Rota. This is that Medicine about which so many have scribbled but so few have known."

INDEX

INDEX

INDEX

Gnosis, 21, 53

Gnostics, 27, 44

God, 14, 18, 22, 24, 26, 28, 29, 30, 31, 40, 46, 47, 48, 49, 50, 56, 57, 69, 70, 72, 73, 75, 80, 81, 82, 86, 87, 94, 95, 97, 103, 104, 107, 112, 113, 114

Gods, The, 6, 22, 23, 27, 53, 54, 55, 56, 58, 71, 72, 73, 74, 76, 109

Gold, 46, 80, 82, 92, 95, 114, 123, 134, 135

Golden Treatise, 127, 132

Gospels, 14

Gospel of Phillip, 120

Great Announcement, 50

Greater World, 90

Great Mother, 88

Great Sea, 88

Great Work, 6, 133

Green Duenech, 90

Green Lion, 37, 82, 90, 132, 133

Green Lizard, 128

Green Stone, 132

Grind, 67

Grimoires, 56, 106

Gross, 63, 78, 131

Gross Body, 35

Gross Work, 86

Gum, 127, 128

H

Heat, 63, 80, 129

Heaven, 10, 22, 75, 82, 87, 96, 97, 111, 118, 120, 135

Hephaestos, 31

HERMES, 23, 28, 31, 37, 68, 70, 118, 120, 127, 132, 133

Hierarchies, 114

Hierophants, 53, 69, 115

HIEROTHEOS, 55

Higher Self, 121

Higher Soul, 94, 95, 97

HIPPOLYTUS, 26, 50

Hot, 130

Humidity, 120

I

IAMBLICHOS, 15, 21, 29, 30, 31, 53. 54, 72, 106

Idolon, 108

Idola, 107, 108

Igneous, 127

Ignis Gehannæ, 36

Imbibe, 67, 76, 122

Impure, 64, 90, 91, 124, 133

Incerate, 67

Initiation, 9, 44, 54

Instrument, 87, 90

Intellect, 49, 116, 117

Intelligence, 22, 23, 28, 29, 31, 55

Intelligible, 77

Invocation, 69, 70, 74, 106

Iron, 83

J

Jacob, 76

Job, 14

K

Kabbale, La, 23, 46

Kabirian Rites, 31

Kerubic Emblem, 37, 128

Key, 38, 62, 63, 86, 87, 88, 119, 122

KHUNRATH, 88, 90, 118

King, 47, 62, 101, 135

KIRCHER, 29

KIRCHRINGIUS, 62, 65, 70

Kneph, 30

Kundalini, 36

L

Laboratory, 129

Land of Havilah, 134

Law, 45, 46, 47, 48

Lead, 83, 90, 105

Lesser World, 89, 101

INDEX

Leo, 37
Light, 24, 30, 31, 36, 58, 62, 74, 75, 87, 94, 103, 115, 116, 123, 124
Lion, 37, 80, 81, 113
Liquefaction, 65
Lizard, 128
Logos, 28
Love, 39, 40, 49, 81, 98
Lower Mind, 20, 27
Lucas, 65
Lully, Raymund, 13, 86, 90, 112, 128
Lumen de Lumine, 39, 112
Luminary, 67

M

Maccabees, 127
Macrocosm, 85, 89, 102
Magia Adamica, 29
Magic, 9, 13, 41, 56, 57, 60, 101, 106, 107
Magical Earth, 133, 134
Magistery, 10, 65, 79, 84
Magnesia, 123, 124, 132, 134
Magus, 57
Male, 39, 50, 51, 82, 103, 135
Manteia, 114
Mantic Trance, 110
Mariette-Bey, 31
Matter, 61, 81, 83, 92, 111, 129
Mead, G. R. S., 27, 44, 50
Medicine, 81, 93, 96, 135, 136
Meditation, 72, 75, 83, 88, 111
Medium, 133
Mekkubalim, 41
Mercurial Water, 120
Mercury, 39, 61, 63, 88, 119, 120, 127, 130
Mercury of the Adepts, 123
Metals, 81, 83
Microcosm, 35, 84, 89, 101
Milk, 80
Milk of Birds, 131
Mind, 19, 20, 22, 23, 24, 27, 28, 31, 33, 39, 49, 50, 51, 73, 74, 94, 101, 103, 111, 117, 124
Minera, 10, 65, 84

Mirandola, Picus de, 10, 57
Mist, 128
Mithra, 9
Moist, 24, 130
Moisture, 40, 129, 130
Mollification, 66
Moon, 56, 80, 111, 124
Morien, 78
Mortification, 36
Mortis Immundities, 36
Moses, 15, 26, 27, 38
Mother, 28, 40, 83, 124
Motion, 63, 124
Mountain, 97, 112, 113
Muesis, 9, 110
Multiplication, 81, 122
Mysteries, 9, 10, 14, 32, 33, 34, 35, 43, 49, 53, 55, 57, 62, 69, 74, 82, 99, 104, 110, 116, 134
Mystery Schools, 9, 15, 33, 53, 115
Mysticism, 6, 53

N

Nature, 13, 57, 59, 66, 77, 81, 82, 89, 96, 101, 102, 111, 119, 123, 124
Neph, 30
Nephesch, 18, 19, 20, 21, 31, 131
Neshamah, 18, 19, 21, 22, 23, 35, 88, 131, 132
New Light of Alchemy, 101
Noesis, 20
Noetic, 21, 33, 110
Norton, Thomas, 57, 69
Nous, 20, 21, 23
Nubia, 30

O

Occult, 6, 7, 31, 44, 66, 117, 123
Occultism, 5, 6
Occult Philosophy, 57, 103
Oil, 133
Oily Tincture, 132, 133
Operation(s), 66, 78, 79, 100, 101, 102, 119, 120, 122

141

INDEX

INDEX

INDEX

CPSIA information can be obtained
at www.ICGtesting.com
Printed in the USA
BVHW040256010223
657580BV00002B/275